LOST DEPARTMENT STORES

of

CLEVELAND

LOST DEPARTMENT STORES *of* CLEVELAND

Michael DeAloia

THE History PRESS

Published by The History Press
Charleston, SC
www.historypress.com

All images courtesy of the Cleveland Press Archives/Cleveland Memory Project unless otherwise noted.

First published 2021

Manufactured in the United States

ISBN 9781467143738

Library of Congress Control Number: 2021931019

This book is dedicated to my daughter—the Wee One—who inspires in me the daily wonder it is to see elements of the world for the very first time. And to my beautiful wife, Nora, who keeps me grounded in the present despite my penchant for living in the past.

CONTENTS

FOREWORD

I don't see Michael DeAloia as often as I would like. Despite the fact that we've known each other for more than a decade now, our meetings are infrequent and invariably delightful. Known for lo these many years as Cleveland's "Tech Czar," to try to label Michael as one thing or another is to do this energetic man of wide interests an injustice. Michael isn't necessarily a Renaissance man, freighted as that word has become with the baggage of centuries. Michael is, quite simply, an exuberant lover of life, family, friends and Cleveland. History isn't history, for Michael, as much as it is an opportunity to share stories that thrill and delight—big events and small happenings.

The mysteries of places lost and people for whom they were significant are recovered by him with the joy of a shepherd with a particularly recalcitrant flock, determined to make him work to uncover their hiding places. And he leaves no stone unturned, as illustrated by his two previous books for Arcadia Publishing and The History Press, *Lost Cleveland: Seven Wonders of the Sixth City* (2010) and *Lost Grand Hotels of Cleveland* (2014). For this reason, it is not surprising that Michael would eventually turn his attention to Cleveland's vanished department stores: Bailey's, Halle's, Higbee's, the May Company, Sterling Lindner and Taylor & Son.

The names Higbee's and the May Company conjure up rich memories of key events in my life. Growing up the youngest child of a peripatetic geologist, I ended up as the new kid, at a new school, for most of my childhood. The summer before third grade, we moved from Livonia, Michigan, to Painesville,

Ohio. I don't remember ever going to downtown Detroit as a child in the 1960s, but I do remember being taken to Cleveland in December 1969 to buy my fifteen-year-old brother a suit. I remember sitting curled up in a chair in Higbee's young men's department, reading Paul Anderson's science fiction fantasy novel *Three Hearts and Three Lions*, not caring if Mother and Father made him try on every suit in the place because it was the school holiday. After all, I had a book I was enjoying, the family was all together and when it got dark, we would go outside in the cold and see the Christmas windows. Everything was magic that Christmas.

I remember visiting Higbee's during another Christmas season, years later in the mid-1980s, as a graduate student at Case Western Reserve University. Along with two friends, both native Clevelanders, we played hooky from class one day and went to have lunch at the then recently restored Silver Grille. They both had memories of dining there as children; I didn't but enjoyed the lunch, and afterward, we had a chat with Bruce the Spruce, the talking Christmas tree, and waved to Mr. Jingeling, the Keeper of the Keys to Santa's Workshop. I don't remember actually purchasing anything in the store, but I remember smelling the perfumes, trying on clothes and riding on the old wooden escalators to the mezzanine and the cheerful *chunkety-chunk* sound the machinery made.

To be fair, my memories are not all of Higbee's. In November 1989, in the last year of my PhD program, my boyfriend of six years proposed to me. One of the loveliest gestures in the months leading up to our wedding in June the following year was the gift of a sum of money in the form of a May Company gift certificate from the students in a Senior Scholars class I taught during the spring semester of 1990. The gift certificate was presented to me on the last day of class, and the following week, I drove out to the old May Company at Severance Mall. On the lower level, in the housewares section, I purchased a set of Paul Revere copper-bottomed pots and pans and two Stiffel lamps—items that were, according to my mother, appropriate purchases for a young couple setting up a new home. In the May Company that day, with those purchases, I left behind the life of a student forever.

For me, and for everyone who experienced them in their various heydays, the grand department stores were always about so much more than retail. Walking through the various departments allowed shoppers and non-shoppers alike to create personal narratives built around whatever was new and exciting—the evening gown, sterling silver charms for a charm bracelet, the pinstripe suit, the porkpie hat, the silk tie, gold cufflinks, a color television or a set of dishes. We looked. Sometimes we bought. Always we imagined.

Michael captures this magic and opportunity in this splendid volume. If you are not old enough to summon up memories of these stores, share the volume with someone who can. Take the time and listen to them reminisce. If you are reading this and recollecting moments of your own, share those too.

The past is richly textured, and for those of us lucky enough to grow up in and around Cleveland in the twentieth century, the great department stores are an integral part of that texture. This is retail therapy—old school—brought to you by one of the most insightful voices on Cleveland history.

—Holly Witchey

Holly Witchey has a PhD in European painting and sculpture and thirty years of experience in museums and higher education. She is currently director of education and outreach at the Intermuseum Conservation Association (ICA) (ica-artconservation.org), the nation's first nonprofit regional art conservation center. In addition to her work with ICA, Dr. Witchey teaches graduate-level museum studies classes for Johns Hopkins University and Case Western Reserve University. In 2016, she launched Cleveland Philanthropy, a small educational 501(c)(3), because she believes that shared inspirational stories have the power to shape the future of urban cultural development.

From 1991 to 1999, Dr. Witchey was associate curator of European art and manager of new media at the San Diego Museum of Art, and from 2000 to 2009, she was director of new media at the Cleveland Museum of Art. Dr. Witchey is the author of Progressive Vision: The History of Downtown Cleveland *(1986) and the coauthor of* The Fine Arts in Cleveland: An Illustrated History *(1994);* An Uncommon Mission *(2000); a mystery,* Cocktail at the Museum*; and, most recently,* The Autobiography of Jeptha Homer Wade: A Modest American. *In 2016, she was named as one of the most interesting people in Cleveland by* Cleveland Magazine.

PREFACE

The decision to write *Lost Department Stores of Cleveland* was finalized on December 28, 2018. I signed my name to a contract with The History Press. This will be my third book written for The History Press—a relationship I have enjoyed for over ten years. That is not to say that signing the contract was not without hesitation or that it held no anxiety. There is always a flood of emotion when one begins the journey to write a book.

Because writing is a lonely exercise. A solo journey into the abyss. A ride down the rabbit hole. The inability to know when night is now day and when day is now night. Sure, your family and friends are around and occasionally knock on your door to inquire how you might be faring. But the act of writing is terribly lonely. I love interacting with people, so writing takes a bit of a toll on me.

Yet, the focus of the book—the long-gone department stores of my favorite city—is endlessly fascinating. Just a little prelude or peek into these wonderful retail shops offers a bit of insight into how grand Cleveland was at its industrial peak. The stores follow the rich history of Cleveland from its humble beginnings as an outpost in the vast Western Reserve of Connecticut to the heady growth of this cold outpost through the Civil War and its industrial underpinnings. Cleveland was at the center of oil, steel, shipping, printing, railroads, textiles, chemicals and, by extension, professional trades like accounting, legal services, private equity and banking. Nearly one million people called this complex city "home," and all needed to buy various assortments of goods, wares and sundries.

The honorable truth is that I am fascinated by the lore, the myth and the legend of the fabulous shopping that once graced Cleveland, and especially Euclid Avenue. The names alone—Higbee's, Halle's, May Company, Taylor Son & Company, Sterling Linder and Bailey's—conjure a comforting memory of sophisticated style and lost glamour. Euclid Avenue, with its dynamic retail stores and homes to countless millionaires, was Cleveland's golden façade. It was of elevated air, considered at one time to be one of a trio of notable retail promenades: Fifth Avenue (New York), State Street (Chicago) and Euclid Avenue.

This is all the more amazing because the original plan for the city did not provide for Euclid Avenue. The once village of Cleveland added the road as a convenience to those traveling to the east. The road was originally surveyed in 1816 and was blessed with the name Euclid as it passed through Euclid Township.[1]

The street followed an old Indian trail and became the route of stagecoaches and freight wagons headed notably for Buffalo and was often called the "Buffalo Road." By 1840, Euclid Avenue was planked with wood, and its destiny as a world-famous avenue was already determined. Not even twenty years later, Euclid was graded. Trees, lawns and gardens were planted. Titans of commerce—Brush, Chisholm, Wade, Rockefeller, King, Wellman, Johnson, Brown and Mather—all took up grand residences on the grand avenue.

The retail stores began as modestly as the city itself. But as the city grew and the wealth of the populace increased—miles and miles of homes owned by the well-to-do and outrageously wealthy began to congregate around Euclid Avenue and Millionaires' Row—Cleveland began to cement itself as a retailer's paradise. A whole gamut of retailers was launched to service the working poor, the growing middle class, the nouveau riche and the old wealth. Each segment of society, it seemed, had its retailer of choice to service it. From daily staples to extraordinary items like furs, demand grew as big and fast as Cleveland itself.

The street would eventually become "the street paved with gold" as many millionaires would wine, dine, conspire, shop and live in luxury along Euclid's corridor. The name itself—Euclid—is derived from Ancient Greek. It means "very glorious" and was the name of a third-century BCE Greek mathematician from Alexandria who made numerous contributions to geometry.[2]

The mighty American department store rose to prominence on the back of rapid industrialization in the late 1800s. As the factories grew in number and output, so did the various railroads—ready to take various products being made to market. More factories meant more people. More people in urban settings. Streetcars made it easy for anyone in the city to get to the core department stores in the downtown area. It was a magical time.

Commerce would slowly creep upon Euclid Avenue as the houses of the wealthy were torn down while office buildings and factories, owned by the very same, took root.

Cleveland's first merchant was Nathan Perry, who sold dry goods beginning in 1809. His retail post was built on "Perry's Corners," now West Ninth Street, and started a retail and trade district that expanded along Superior Street (now Avenue) to Public Square.

From 1815 until the 1830s, Cleveland's retail businesses were clustered on Superior Street west of Public Square, while the square itself was almost entirely surrounded by private dwellings. Cleveland's geography was a blessing that brought the Erie Canal terminus into the city. Post–Civil War, the city became the crossroads of America for many railroad companies. Cleveland's industrial base prospered, and all of this changed the evolutionary course of Cleveland's retail industry.

By 1860, Cleveland's vibrant retail center was located west of Public Square and clustered around West Sixth Street. When Hower & Higbee (eventually just Higbee's) announced in the Cleveland newspapers that it was going to build a new store on West Third Street, it was considered a bit of a scandal. Cleveland's first department store was McGillin's on Superior Street near Public Square. McGillin's immediate neighbor was Paddock & Sons Furriers & Hatters. In 1892, the impressive Halle brothers took over the Paddock retail store, beginning Halle's amazing run as Cleveland's high-end retail store. In the spring of 1870, William Taylor and Thomas Kilpatrick launched Taylor Kilpatrick and Company on the Cushing Block at the southeast corner of Public Square. The giants of Cleveland retail were beginning to take root. The Taylor Kilpatrick store is notable, too, for a different reason. Dr. Erastus Cushing persuaded the two young entrepreneurs to locate their store on Euclid Avenue. The commercial conquest of Euclid Avenue was beginning.

It should be noted that a very vibrant (and not well-known) seed of Cleveland retail success was planted in 1898. In this year, the Cleveland Retail Credit Men's Company was organized in November during a luncheon discussion at the Chamber of Commerce Building. It was the first merchant-owned cooperative and nonprofit credit bureau in the United States and possibly the world. As the credit accounts grew in number (and

Cleveland was experiencing explosive growth during this period of time), the merchants decided that pooling credit experiences and having a central credit exchange would benefit all merchants.

Started by a few retailers and merchants, two thousand businesses and financial institutions were to share the benefits for many decades. Top retailers at the time—including Hower & Higbee, Strauss Bros., Davis & Company and W.H. Quimby—were instrumental in creating this world-class group by sharing retail data. This was an unheard-of compromise by so many businesses. In fact, the larger department stores in Cleveland all shared a charge card until the May Company decided to leave the charge card consortium and announced its own charge card in July 1966. Sure, the Big Six retail giants of Cleveland were competitors, but more often than not they cooperated well with one another.

Cleveland at the turn of the twentieth century was a booming, wealthy city but not a particularly pretty one.[3] By the early 1900s, it was becoming abundantly clear that Euclid Avenue was going to become the grand retail boulevard. In 1910, Halle Brothers Department Store shocked the powers that be in Cleveland by announcing its new store would be "uptown" from Public Square and Superior Avenue and would be built on Euclid Avenue near East Twelfth Street. The momentum had now moved to Euclid Avenue (as the street was now moving away from Millionaires' Row to the Miracle Mile of retail stores). Other stores soon followed, including specialty stores like Cowell & Hubbard, Sterling Welch and eventually Higbee's.

The city's golden age (1890–1930) witnessed unprecedented economic growth and construction activity. Cleveland's population grew from 261,353 in 1890 to 381,768 in 1900 to 560,663 in 1910 to 796,841 in 1920 to an astounding 900,429 in 1930. All of these hearty souls needed to buy dry goods, fresh food and clothing. With this rapid increase in population came a proliferation of retail stores. The number of dry good stores in Cleveland jumped from 20 in 1860 to 200 in 1900 to 504 in 1920. As more Cleveland families acquired wealth, retailers began to position themselves to meet the demand from basic commodities to luxury goods.[4]

Historians would realize that 1910 had been the last year that all but a dozen new department stores were established in the United States. As a retail species, they were born almost exclusively between 1860 and 1910. The future of the breed would be one of expansion or consolidation.[5] And yet of the types of retail stores, the large and famous department stores were, in my opinion, the most exciting form of retailing. The economic vitality of department stores was matched by their social influence.

Safe to say that by 1915, the department stores that would dominate Cleveland retailing (and future generations' imaginations) until the early 1960s—Taylor Son & Company, Bailey's, May, Higbee, Halle and Sterling-Linder—were firmly entrenched downtown. And by the 1920s, national retail chains—S.S. Kresge, F.W. Woolworth, McCory, W.T. Grant, Bond, Richman Brothers, Bonwit Teller and Sears—began to build impressive stores in the Sixth City. Downtown Cleveland was the mecca of retail. In fact, Cleveland was one of the largest shopping districts in the United States.

The greatest retail shopping season of all for the downtown department stores was, of course, Christmas. Every store created a special version of the holiday spirit all along Euclid Avenue. All the department stores decorated for the season, including (but certainly not limited to) Higbee's, Halle's, May Company, Sterling Linder, the Bond Store and many others. Hough Bakeries, too, created a cornucopia of holiday treats and delights at all of its stores. During the holidays, one could find petits fours, canapes, fruitcakes and sugar cookies waiting at Hough Bakeries.[6] For years, the city held a gigantic Christmas parade in downtown Cleveland. The annual parade drew big crowds, and big names performed at the event, including Johnny Mathis and the Jackson 5. Nela Park, too, was a Christmas adventure. The business estate owned by General Electric created a drive-through park every year during the holidays—the "Winter Wonder Land of Lights."

The department store was a celebration of American exceptionalism. These coveted structures are where any man, woman and child could go and dream of a better life. Under a single roof, one could buy furniture, clothing, carpets, hats, gloves, books, gift cards, electronics and exotic goods. Many would get their hair cut at the department store barbershop or hair salon. Generations of children would dress in their Sunday best to partake in a now fading rite—the department store lunch.[7]

There was an elegance and panache that emanated from the department store. Post–World War II, the Cleveland department stores became the focal point of women's fashion, with all of them holding regular luncheon fashion shows in their auditoriums to exhibit the finest collections from the day's most important designers.[8] The American lifestyle after World War II changed dramatically as families moved away from their urban roots and into the suburbs (a trend that is only now beginning to shift back to the urban environments). The superhighways, the proliferation of the automobile and the shopping center phenomenon put severe pressure on the downtown department store and gave rise to the multi-anchored department stores for a regional mall or shopping center.

By 1971, Halle's had become a division of Marshall Field. That left Higbee's as the only major independent department store in Cleveland. And by the end of the 1990s, none of the Bix Six Cleveland department stores was still in operation—although Higbee's existed as Dillard's until 2002.[9]

Then the world tilted yet again in the 1990s, and department stores began to disappear from our neighborhoods, from our drive home and ultimately from our consciousness. May turned into Kaufmann's, Higbee's turned into Dillard's, Bailey turned into Neville's (at least part of it), Halle's went out of business, Sterling Linder was closed and Taylor Son & Company seemingly just disappeared. Retail in Cleveland had entered the dark ages. The decline also involved the small specialty retailers. In 1972, the upscale Bonwit Teller store on Playhouse Square was briefly converted into an outlet store. Other women's fashion shops, like the Peck & Peck and Engle & Fetzer, also closed. Prominent jewelers on Euclid Avenue like Webb C. Bell and Cowell & Hubbard succumbed to the retail exodus.[10]

Today, downtown Cleveland is enjoying a grand renewal. The city is rich with restaurants, theaters, sports and living. Many of the old buildings downtown, like the old Taylor Son and Halle buildings, have been turned into apartments. New life for old buildings. While retail has been a larger challenge in downtown, Cleveland does have a new grocery store—Heinen's—and a small department store. In 2015, Geiger's opened its downtown store in the old Truman Building on Euclid Avenue (next to the Heinen's). It is the third store for the eighty-seven-year-old chain that is based in Lakewood, Ohio, and once competed against Bailey's department store. More retail is expected in downtown as more and more apartments are built and more people (predominantly millennials and empty nesters) reclaim urban living. There is no doubt that, if they were still alive today, the owners of Higbee's or Halle's or even Sterling Linder would have reveled in the reemergence of Cleveland and its dynamic downtown.

ACKNOWLEDGEMENTS

Despite my lamenting that writing a book is a lonely exercise, no one ever writes a book alone. Especially a book of history. There are so many people to thank for guiding me through this journey. It all starts with John Rodrigue at The History Press. John was insanely supportive and eloquently persistent in getting me to write my third book for the Press. Kudos, John.

Big thanks to the Lakewood Historical Society for all the great detail on the Bailey's store in Lakewood. Good folks at the society include Greg Palumbo, director, and Pamela Dorazio Dean, curator. The society recently moved into a new facility to house its archives and public resources. If ever in the great city of Lakewood, Ohio, stop in for a visit to the archives. They would be happy to show you around.

The great lineage of Cleveland historians starts with Samuel Peter Orth, glides to William Ganson Rose, extends to David Van Tassel and is now carried by John Grabowski. What I wouldn't do to be in that great list of Cleveland historians. I am eternally indebted to John Grabowski for his time, his deep knowledge and his valuable friendship. I could never have finished a single book, much less three, without John's help. And a big thank-you to Ann Sindelar, also of the Western Reserve Historical Society, for letting me stop by one rainy spring Saturday morning to finish a little research on some choice photos and blueprints. This book is better for it.

As any writer will attest, during my research phase for the book I happened to go down a rabbit hole (a joyous trip into a whole new set of photos) that led me to Wetzler's Photography. Much to my surprise (and happiness), Wetzler's had an entire section of its website devoted to historical photos of Cleveland, Ohio. I emailed the company, and the next morning, Margaret Wetzler replied. She could not have been more helpful. In fact, one night she delivered the entire Wetzler's historical archive to my office in Lakewood, Ohio. (Turns out we both live in the city. Small world.) The archive is robust, remarkable and stunning. The photos show a Cleveland from a different time with a much different look.

Bill Barrow, head of the special collections at the Michael Schwartz Library at Cleveland State University, is a rare human being. He possesses some of the deepest knowledge of Cleveland history, which he gives away freely to anyone with a keen interest in learning more about the Sixth City. Under his protection are the Cleveland Press archives and the Cleveland Memory Project. Both are rich with photos and stories from Cleveland's amazingly deep and fascinating past. A lot of the photos in this book are found at the Cleveland Memory Project. And with that said, thank you to Vern Morrison for searching the Cleveland Memory archives and turning the old photos into the crisp images you see in this book.

Sometimes the world works in funny ways, and the story about how I connected with Cindy Halle is too convoluted to even attempt an explanation. But I am deeply indebted to Cindy for giving me some time to talk in detail about the Halle family and especially her husband, Chisholm Halle, who died too young at the age of forty-eight.

A big thanks to all my family and friends who were supportive to me during the writing of *Lost Department Stores of Cleveland*. I would not have been able to get this book finished if it weren't for the help and moral support of the Evergreen Podcasts (www.evergreenpodcasts.com) family. It is an honor to work with the best podcast company and production talent ever assembled. Thank you, David Allen Moss, Doug Trostler, Brigid Coyne, Conor Standish, Paige Koteles, Julie Fink, Dave Douglas, Eric Koltnow, Sarah Willgrube and Hannah Leach. Of course, a big thank-you must go to Joan Andrews, the founder of Evergreen Podcasts, for allowing me and the entire Evergreen team to feed our creativity.

And thank you to my mother-in-law, Lynn Loftus, who inspired me with personal stories of being an elevator operator at Higbee's back in the early 1950s. From the white gloves and snappy uniform to the after-hour drinks with other Higbee employees, her affection for the glory days of Cleveland's department stores is quite contagious.

Finally, a few short, sweet words to my wife, Nora (who helped with editing the book), and my lovely little daughter, Ileana. I love you both.

A Few Key Links

Cleveland Press Archives: www.clevelandmemory.org/press
Cleveland Public Library: www.cpl.org
Lakewood Historical Society: www.lakewoodhistory.org
Western Reserve Historical Society: www.wrhs.org
Wetzler's Photography: www.wetzlers.com

THE BAILEY COMPANY

The Store for All the People

The History

The hustle and bustle of the big city was intoxicating to two entrepreneurs who aspired to be retail titans. The two gentlemen—Lewis Bailey and Joseph Crothers—pooled their resources and knowledge to open the L.A. Bailey Dry Goods Company in 1881. The store was opened on the corner of Ontario Street and Prospect Avenue a block from Cleveland's famed Public Square and was a welcomed addition to the retail landscape.

Bailey and Crothers selected a location that had a deep history as a retail center. In 1837, the Farmers Block, a merchandising center established on this same corner, was built to draw trade from the countryside.[11] Also on this same corner in 1858, the Burnett House, a hotel and event venue, began to host weddings, reunions and festive occasions. The House increased in popularity and soon was enlarged. In 1867, it was improved and opened as the Cleveland Hotel. A series of landlords moved in until about 1880, when John B. White leased the hotel and renamed it the Prospect House. Colonel Ransom A. Gillette took it over a year later, and for more than a decade, it flourished. It was renamed the Wilmont in 1893 and then the Hotel Frankfurt, and in 1905, the Bailey Company acquired the location and spent the next couple of decades building and rebuilding until the old structure disappeared.[12]

Bailey's East Side store on Euclid Avenue near University Circle (1949).

Bailey's proved a very successful small shop and grew rapidly. The two owners decided in 1895 to expand into a five-story structure flush with dry goods and added a grocery department. The new shop included modern improvements such as iron elevators, electric lighting and new ventilation. The store was a phenomenon, but the hard work necessary to keep the bustling enterprise on the rails was beginning to take its toll on Lewis Bailey. After eighteen years of creating the American dream for himself and his family, Bailey fell into bad heath and passed away in 1899. He was beloved and was known as a natural salesman—a talent one would most definitely need to possess to build a thriving retail chain.

Colonel Louis Black and Charles K. Sunshine soon thereafter bought out Bailey's equity and merged the Bailey's store into the Cleveland Dry Goods Company.[13] After the merger, Bailey's retained eleven veteran retail employees. The remaining two owners focused on customer service and improved the selection of products. In 1903, Bailey's updated its original five-story structure with a gorgeous seven-story improvement, including a stunning Mansard roof (a type of roof having two slopes on every side, the lower slope being considerably steeper than the upper). Times were good for the old dry good store, and the company's sales were prodigious. According to longtime Cleveland chronicler William Ganson Rose, the key to Bailey's success was its knack for enticing solid crowds with reasonable prices:

> *Bailey's Department store in 1905 offered a number of specials for men. Derby hats were sold at 95 cents, and caps and hats were priced at from 15 cents to $1.90. All-wool suits and overcoats in the latest fabrics, usually $10 to $12, were offered for $6.80; stiff or soft bosom shirts were sold for thirty nine cents and kids gloves for forty nine cents. Overalls were priced at thirty five cents, corduroy pants at twenty nine cents for children and ordinary school pants at fifteen cents.*[14]

Bailey's success continued, and in 1910, they built an additional ten-story building right next to the May Company expansion on Ontario Street (discussed later in this book). A fine addition to the new structure was the Bailey's Soda Fountain, where shoppers could enjoy a fine lunch and homemade ice cream.

Bailey's was one of the first department stores to expand its store concept to other parts of Cleveland proper. As the city grew and expanded, so did Bailey's. Bailey's was the first Cleveland department store to operate both east and west side branches. In 1929, Bailey's built its first branch store in the University Circle area of Cleveland. This store was located at 10007 Euclid Avenue near what is now the Cleveland Clinic. Other stores followed: Lakewood in 1930, Euclid in 1951 and Mayfield Heights

Bailey's Eastgate Shopping Center at SOM Center and Mayfield Road. Going out of business (1967).

New customers in Bailey's new branch store at East 228th Street and Lake Shore Boulevard, Euclid, Ohio (1951).

in 1959. To support this growth, Bailey's leased 125,000 square feet of warehouse space on Dodge Court in downtown Cleveland. The frontage to this warehouse was 1375 Euclid Avenue, which is now the IdeaStream Building at Playhouse Square.

Given the success of Bailey's, the company's board and President Victor W. Sincere decided in 1927 to form a new company called National Department Stores. All of Bailey's assets were given to National Department Stores, and it was made a division of the new company. National Department then acquired other local and regional chains and essentially let them operate as separate divisions.

Bailey's continued to flourish even as a small cog in a much larger organization. The department store soon became a prime target for acquisition, especially for another enterprise considering building a national retail company by cobbling together a number of regional department store chains. Bailey's parent corporation, National Department Stores, had come to the conclusion in 1955 that the golden era of retailers was over and subsequently announced that it was going to divest itself of all of its retail operations, which consisted at the time of Bailey's, Rosenbaum Company and Frank & Soder in Pittsburgh. The National Department Stores board decided that the next big industry to invest in was energy, and thus it was considered the ideal time to shed retail assets and begin buying mining and drilling operations. The company changed its name to the International Mining Company.

In 1958, the Century Food Market (CFM) Company bought Bailey's with the idea to make Bailey's the largest department store in Cleveland. CFM was a Youngstown, Ohio–based grocery store chain with twenty-six stores. At the time of the transaction, it was estimated that Bailey's had $13 million in revenue and CFM had $32 million in revenue.[15]

CFM traced its origins back to 1917, when Russian immigrants Samuel and Dina Aron opened a small grocery store in Youngstown.[16] Jules Aron was now the CEO of CFM and was a very astute executive. CFM itself was acquired by Loblaw, Inc., the Buffalo, New York division of the Canadian retailer Loblaw. The fourth store in the chain was approved by CFM in 1959. CFM retained famed Cleveland, Ohio developer Anthony Visconsi of Visconsi & Associates to build the new seventy-five-thousand-square-foot facility.[17] Before the sale of Bailey's to CFM, it was rumored that the chain was going to be sold to Federal's, a Detroit-based retail chain that had opened some stores in the Cleveland area and was looking to add additional stores inexpensively. But CFM won with an aggressive bid on Bailey's assets.

In 1961, CFM made a series of fatally bad decisions regarding Bailey's operation. First, the company's CEO, Jules Aron, announced layoffs at every store. Then the CFM board in early 1962 revealed that it was closing the iconic downtown Bailey's flagship store and its uptown location at Euclid Avenue and East 101st Street. Bailey's next-door neighbor, the May Company, quickly purchased the Bailey building and set about demolishing the structure in 1964. In its place, May built a multistory Parkade, which offered May Company shoppers a covered parking area with direct access to the still lavish May Company shopping experience. The Parkade also included a tire and automotive service center at the street level. The 200,000-square-foot garage could park eight hundred cars and was expected to handle three thousand cars daily.[18] This structure is still standing today on the corner of Ontario Street and Huron Road.

At the time of the downtown and uptown store closings, CFM hired the venerable Ostendorf-Morris commercial real estate firm to search for other suburban opportunities to build new Bailey department stores. The

Department heads at Bailey's Euclid store. *Left to right*: Alfred Yule, Lillian Fredericks Greenstein, John Gallagher, Henry A. Friedman, Ione Marshall, Fred Culp, Mary Cochran, Paul J. Ockerman, Allan H. Blackstone, Jerry Osborne and manager Fred Koenig (1951).

president of Bailey's noted, "There will always be a downtown, but we feel our future is in the suburbs."[19] But no suburban stores were ever built.

The closing of the downtown Bailey's angered many in Cleveland. There were letters to the editor in both daily newspapers. Strong civic condemnation by various political leaders and numerous patrons of the store demonstrated their disapproval by not shopping at the other Bailey stores. This, of course, had a negative effect on revenue, and CFM came up with a quick resolution of opening a smaller Bailey's store on Prospect Avenue. In the fall of 1962, Bailey's opened the first two floors of its new eleven-story building located at 514 Prospect Avenue. The building formerly housed the Bing Furniture Company. By the early 1960s, Prospect Avenue had a cemented reputation as a low-end retail street. This move to Prospect Avenue further diminished Bailey's reputation as a quality retailer.

CFM's numerous operational mistakes created financial stress for the Bailey chain. CFM decided to sell its problems away and in 1963 merged the

Bailey's chain with Miracle Mart. Executives at Miracle Mart were rather enthusiastic with the Bailey's chain and promised to improve the chain's product mix and implement new pricing strategies, none of which helped generate new revenue for the troubled department store. In 1968, in what can only be called a disastrous decision, the Miracle Mart board decided to close and remodel the Euclid, Mayfield Heights and downtown stores and reopen them as Bailey's Wonder Marts. The Lakewood store had been sold to the Neville's Department Store chain in 1965.

Bailey's Wonder Marts were a last-gasp attempt to compete with the growing discount retail chain phenomenon in the late 1960s. The discount chains offered fewer frills and lower prices than their department store cousins. Value was now more important than quality and service, things that Bailey's excelled at. The up-and-coming discount chains at the time included Zayre's, K-Mart, Bradlee's and Uncle Bill's. The new model at Bailey's, however, failed to attract new customers, and revenues continued to decline. Soon after launching the Wonder Mart concept, Bailey's declared bankruptcy.

Bailey Company downtown Cleveland department store located on Ontario Street and Prospect Avenue (1949).

Bailey Company downtown Lakewood brand store at Detriot Avenue and Warren Road (1949).

The Bailey's Department Store was a first-class four-story department store located on the southeast corner of Detroit Avenue and Warren Road (1933).

Bailey's was never a lavish or spectacular department store. Its product mix and service offerings were tailored to working-class joes and frugal middle-class shoppers. It truly was a department store for the people. The department store offered a number of innovations throughout its history. The store was one of the early innovators of store charge cards and installment plans, for example.

During the early days of the company, immigrants were heavily courted by Bailey's. In fact, the store hired a number of interpreters who manned the sales stations. Working at Bailey's was a career—not a summer job. The store promoted its employees from the low ranks of cashier and stock boy to the middle-class jobs of store buyer and department manager. It's true that Bailey's competed more with the discount chains than its white shoe department store cousins like Higbee's, Halle's or May. But that should not mute Bailey's luster as a Cleveland department store original.

The Store

Bailey's—Euclid, Ohio

Bailey's opened its Euclid branch on November 23, 1951. Executives at Bailey had carefully planned the development of the store. This included hiring the well-respected architects Weinberg & Teare. The architectural firm could trace its roots to Joseph Weinberg, who began his architectural practice in 1919. Weinberg's practice flourished and was known by a number of names, but by 1949, the original architectural firm was named Weinberg & Teare. The firm had built a number of historical buildings in Cleveland, including the Lakeview Terrace complex (which was completed in 1937 and hailed at the time as a landmark public housing development), the Chesterfield Apartments, Lakeview Towers and the Jewish Community Federation Building in downtown Cleveland.

The architects designed the Bailey's building in yellow brick and concrete with a generous amount of glass for patrons to see the goods inside the store. The storefront ran 140 feet along Lake Shore Boulevard and extended 250 feet deep on East 228th Street. The multistory building offered a lower level, which housed the home furnishings as well as appliances, fabrics/linens and bedsheets. The street-level area housed the shoe department, men's, women's and children's clothing, a drugstore and greeting cards. The mezzanine area featured various service departments, a beauty salon and

Looking northeast across Warren Road at the new extension on the Bailey's Department Store on the southeast corner of Detroit and Warren Road (1964).

the credit department. To talk with an experienced Bailey representative, all one had to do was call RE 1-9200.

Bailey's was well received in Euclid and was the city's first department store. The Bailey's chain was acquired by Miracle Mart in 1966. As part of the purchase, the Euclid branch was closed for a few months for extensive remodeling and reopened on March 9, 1969, as Bailey's Wonder Mart. The new department store concept was not well received, and the Euclid brand of Bailey's closed with the rest of the stores in 1969.

Bailey's—Lakewood, Ohio

> *The new Bailey Co. store, itself a definite contribution to the prosperity of Lakewood, and with other merchants have set the pace for Lakewood business and prosperity.*
> *—E.A. Wiegand, mayor of Lakewood*

By 1930, the population of Lakewood was 70,509. The city was the densest urban area in the state of Ohio. And it was a lacking a robust retail marketplace. For years, there were rumors that the Detroit Avenue and Warren Road intersection (and the center of downtown Lakewood) would become a mecca of retail for residents of Lakewood and the West Shore who were thirsting for new shopping experiences. When Bailey's announced

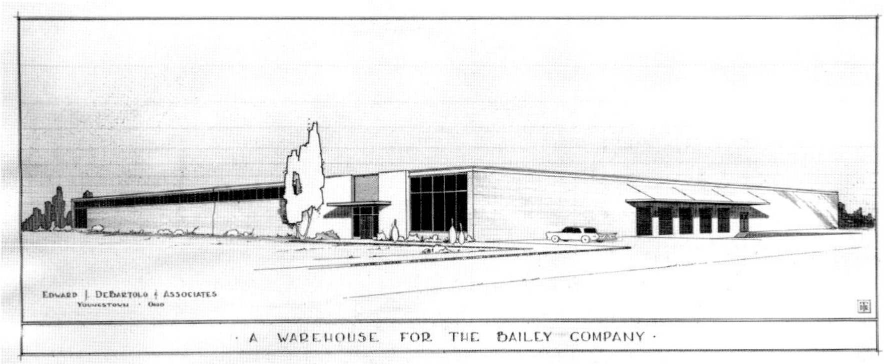

Top: The new Bailey Department Store warehouse design. The building had 101,500 square feet of floor space to service Bailey's five department stores in the Cleveland area (1960).

Bottom: This photo shows the Bailey Department Store and the May Company buildings (both on Ontario) before the construction of the Terminal Tower complex (1925).

that it would be opening a store on the southeast corner of Detroit and Warren, it essentially marked a retail renaissance for Lakewood.

The corners of Detroit Avenue and Warren Road are of great historical significance to the city of Lakewood. Pioneer James Nicholson settled west of the Cuyahoga River in what was then known as Rockport in 1812. In 1820,

Mars Wagar bought a tract of land adjoining Nicholson's in 1820, and the two men began a close friendship. Wagar worked his land well and realized significant profits from his real estate transactions. The Wagar homestead site at the "corners"—Warren Road and Detroit Avenue—became the home of the Bailey Company store in Lakewood.[20]

In fact, following the Bailey's Lakewood announcement, a number of retail shops began building or renting space near the new department store. As detailed in the April 10, 1930 edition of the *Lakewood Post*:

> *Just previously Fournier had moved into a smarter shop. Bernsee followed suit by outfitting an extremely attractive shoe store. Carl Zwierlein took a lease on one of the new stores and announced his intention of bringing his years of shoe merchandising experience into the district. Murray Jones, head of the Jones shops in Cleveland, leased one of the new storerooms and announced a pretentious Lakewood branch. A large furniture store is another of the impending developments. The Lakewood Savings and Loan built a new and finer building. The Belle Square Flower shop moved to a more commodious store. There are others—there will be many others. Lease prices have risen sharply and there is not a landlord who could not lease many additional stores at an attractive figure.*[21]

L.G. Oppenheim, general manager of the Lakewood branch, presented a gold key to the mayor of Lakewood, who then presented a proclamation. Bailey's added a lot of hustle and bustle to Lakewood's new retail district. The corner of Detroit Avenue and Warren Road would eventually include the Bailey department store, Carson's women's fashion store, two dime stores, a Fanny Farmer's candy store, a hardware store and two drugstores. Like at the Euclid branch, to talk directly to a Bailey's store representative, all one had to do was call AC 6-2860.

The original store had four floors completely equipped to give efficient, courteous and abundant service:

Main-Floor Departments

Men's Clothing • Men's Shoes • Men's Hats • Boys' Clothing • Women's Handbags • Silks and Linens

Second-Floor Departments

Women's Dresses • Women's Millinery • Women's and Children's Shoes • Restrooms • Will Call

Third-Floor Departments
Rugs and Carpets • Furniture • Lamps • Radio • Alterations • Manager's Office • Credit Offices

Basement Departments
Curtains and Draperies • Blankets • Sewing Machines • Hardware • Toys • Refrigerators • Washing Machines

That Bailey's selected Lakewood as its first West Side location is a bit curious. Certainly, the executives at Bailey's thought that the city was undeserved. It was the third-largest city in Cuyahoga County behind Cleveland and Parma. However, Lakewood already was home to a well-known and much beloved department store: Schermer Brother's. The original Schermer store opened in 1906 on Madison Avenue in what was then called the Carbon District.[22] The initial Schermer's opened as a very generic clothing store. It was operated by an immigrant couple from Hungary, Abraham and Gussie Greenwald. In 1918, the Greenwalds needed help managing the store and sent for help from their families in Hungary. Isadore and Joseph Schermer answered the call. A couple of years later, the department store was officially renamed Schermer Brothers.

By 1924, Schermer's boasted a three-story building offering patrons nearly thirty thousand square feet of retail bliss. The store was well stocked with dry goods, shoes, household furnishings, kids' clothing, toys, hardware and appliances. The Schermers could speak the Slavic languages found in the neighborhoods around the store, and the immigrant families adored the store and its owners.

In 1962, a catastrophic fire enveloped the Schermer department store. It took Lakewood firemen nearly twelve hours to contain the blaze. The whole store was lost. And then, to add insult to injury, a few days after the fire, Lakewood experienced a brutal wind storm that whipped up off Lake Erie and blew down the store's lone remaining wall. The family rallied and opened a much smaller retail store nearby at 12221 Madison Avenue that operated until 1970.[23]

Bailey's renovated its Lakewood store in 1955. The remodeling project centered on the installation of an imported natural rose granite storefront along the façade and the improvement of store floor planning to improve the actual floor space of the store. After the renovation, Bailey's improved the number of items for sale in the store. The former two-door entrance gave way to an attractive, voluminous center entrance done completely in glowing aluminum and glass.[24]

By 1964, Bailey's had grown from its single store downtown to four established stores in Cleveland (downtown, Lakewood, Euclid and Eastgate) and five stores in the Youngstown area, which were added after the acquisition of Bailey's by Youngstown-based CFM. The whole chain would receive a face-lift, including the Lakewood store. The official announcement of store improvements came in 1963, when Irwin Ware, the president of Bailey's, told the *Plain Dealer* of the chain's improvement plan.

The Lakewood improvement plan completely transformed the store at a cost of $1 million. The store had been enlarged by an addition to the back of the original department store structure. This three-floor adjunct (eight thousand square feet of space per floor) helped with the expansion of a number of departments within the store.[25] There was a new entrance, a new elevator and a stairway accessible from the store's enlarged attached parking garage. Even the sidewalks received some new features in the form of a high-tech snow-melting system embedded in the sidewalks. The entire façade of the building was given a thorough modernization and redecorating program. A new, "modern" façade of pre-cast concrete elements gave the old building the look of a Brutalist structure that tucked nicely against the INA Building that was being constructed at the time next door.

Miracle Mart decided in 1964 to update the Lakewood store. An additional twenty-four thousand square feet were acquired in the newly constructed INA Building next door. Other improvements to the Lakewood store included a new second-story entrance into a new adjoining garage, a new glowing white façade added to the original building and an expanded men's department. Needing cash for its other retail operations, Miracle Mart sold the Bailey's Lakewood store to Neville's in 1965.

Neville's formally opened on February 1, 1965, and took over the landmark space that Bailey's had occupied for more than thirty-four years. The company was headed by C. Stephen Babin, a former furrier and now a real estate developer, and Ernest M. Knapp, a private investor. Both men were from Lakewood and owned the entire block of buildings and parking structures where Neville's was located. The men had purchased the building for $1 million from Bailey's prior to the close of the department store. After Bailey's declared the store closed, the men purchased the business and inventory for an additional $500,000. They retained nearly one hundred employees from the Bailey's store, and John Vannell remained on as store manager. It was a noble start for the new department store company.

The store had a modest expansion in early 1966. Neville's added seven thousand new square feet on the street level going into the new INA Building (which was finishing up construction at this time) and ten thousand square feet of additional space in the downstairs area. This expansion cost $200,000.[26] Neville's closed in 1968 with little notice or fanfare. After the store's closing, the *Lakewood Sun-Post* newspaper held a contest to see which store the suburb would like to see take over the former Bailey's store. Many of the department stores in this book were mentioned, as well as other national department stores like Sears and JCPenney. But the city of Lakewood could never convince another chain to take Bailey's place.

Bailey's—Uptown

The Bailey Company announced on April 14, 1929, that it would be building its first branch store in the Uptown District, or Doan's Corner, in Cleveland. The building was a three-story structure with a full basement containing roughly forty thousand square feet of retail space. The building was owned by Acme Realty Company. The lease was negotiated by Central National Bank, and the attorneys involved in the transaction were Mooney, Hahn, Loeser & Keough (now Hahn Loeser). Doan's Corner was a well-known entertainment district and widely considered Cleveland's "second downtown." The area was blessed with numerous theaters—the Park, Keith's East 105th, the Circle (famed in its own right as the first venue north of the Mason-Dixon line to present Elvis Presley in concert), the University and the Alhambra. Doan's Corner also was the home of Case Institute of Technology and Western Reserve University, not to mention the Cleveland Art Museum and soon Severance Hall, home of Cleveland's world-famous orchestra.

After World War II, management at Bailey's decided it was time to update and modernize its store in the Uptown district. In 1945, the lease of the store was extended to 1955 (with an option for an additional five years). The store was seen as too small for the "modern shopper," so the company bought the Laurel Building next door, thus doubling the retail footprint of the original Bailey's store in Uptown.

The Characters

Colonel Louis Black

The good Colonel was a well-respected civic and business leader involved in numerous endeavors in Cleveland but is best known as the president of the Bailey Company. Black was a native of Hungary and immigrated to Cleveland in 1854. To prove his patriotism to his new country, he joined the 150th Ohio Volunteer Infantry Regiment.[27] His initial business foray was in the D. Black Cloak Company, where he retained his business interest until 1896. In 1899, he partnered with Charles K. Sunshine to acquire the controlling interest in the Bailey department store. Black remained with the store as president and treasurer until his death in 1919.

Black served two years on Cleveland City Council and was quite active in Republican politics. Curiously, he became the city's first ever fire director under then-mayor William Grey Rose. He was a longtime member of the Cleveland Grays, an independent volunteer militia to aid the state from any military incursions. His love of the Grays ran deep as he became a trustee during the militia's drive to build the Grays Armory (which still exists today).

Bailey's west side branch in Lakewood with a new façade (1964).

A photo of Bailey's Department store taken prior to the Terminal Tower being constructed (year not listed). *Courtesy of Wetzler's Photography.*

His title of Colonel, it seems, was honorific and acquired from his membership in the Knights of Pythias. The Knights of Pythias was founded during the Civil War in Washington, D.C., and was the first fraternal organization to be chartered by an act of Congress. The group was founded on the legend of Damon and Pythias, a Greek story of honor and friendship. Membership in the organization required a belief in a supreme being and was open to men in good health. According to the secret rituals of the organization, when a man was inducted into the group, he received a ceremonial sword usually bearing the letters FCB, which stood for Friendship, Charity, Benevolence—the three attributes of the organization.

Black had additional business interests in banking and real estate. He was married to his wife, Anna, for fifty-one years and had two children, Roy Black and Mrs. Victor Sincere. Mr. Victor Sincere was the president of Bailey's and instrumental in forming the National Department Stores company.

Jules Aron

The lineage to the Century Food Mart started in 1917 when Russian immigrants Samuel and Diana Aron opened a small grocery on Chicago Avenue in Youngstown. Jules was born in 1919. The four sons of Samuel and Diana—Fador, Harry, Julius (Jules to his family and friends) and Norman—founded the Century Food Market chain in 1940. The brothers had anticipated that self-serve supermarkets would eventually supplant mom-and-pop shops in neighborhoods. In addition to Youngstown, the family operated stores in Warren, Berea and Ellwood City, Pennsylvania.[28] Soon, the company expanded in Greater Akron, adding locations at Arlington Plaza, Wooster-Hawkins Plaza, Coventry Plaza, 866 West Wilbeth Road in Akron, 655 West Portage Trail in Cuyahoga Falls, University Plaza in Kent and finally Lakemore Plaza. Takeover rumors began to circulate in 1960, and by May 1961, Jules and his brothers had sold the chain to Loblaw Inc.

HALLE BROS. COMPANY

A Gift from Halle's Means More

THE HISTORY

One of Cleveland's most famous department stores had a very humble beginning. The doors of the Halle Bros. store opened on February 7, 1891. Two Halle brothers, Salmon Portland and Samuel Horatio—known in the store by their initials S.P. and S.H.—acquired the T.S. Paddock & Company hat and furrier shop at 221 Superior Avenue.[29] The modest store, a mere 25 by 220 feet, held court on an avenue that was once Cleveland's retail center. The store's stock was limited to hats, caps and furs. Its specialty was "railroad" and "society" caps made to order. How could these young men know at the time that they would play a critical role in transforming Cleveland from an awkward, adolescent factory town to a sophisticated, mature metropolis?

Cleveland exemplified the American mystique realized by the hard work, the sweat on the proverbial brow and the great sacrifice of an immigrant population. And the story of Halle's is no different. The first Halle to make it to Cleveland was Aaron Halle, who left Bavaria in 1842.[30] He somehow found passage on a boat that stopped at almost every small port along the Lake Erie coast. When Aaron finally landed in Cleveland, the city's population was only 6,077 people. Only 200 of those families were European immigrants, predominantly Irish or German, and of these, only 20 were Jewish.

Aaron Halle decided to become a grocer and opened a very basic grocery store. He sold mostly dry goods but some fresh produce and meats, too. He

Halle's mall entrance at Severance Center (1982).

knew that some of his family desperately wanted to leave Germany and come to America. So after saving a dollar here and there, Aaron sent money to his cousin Manuel Halle. Manuel followed the same route as Aaron, navigating his way across the Atlantic, taking the canals to Buffalo and booking a ship from Buffalo to Cleveland. It was now Manuel's turn to save money and then send for his brother Moses. By the time Moses got to Cleveland in 1848, the city had doubled its population and was becoming an important cog in the Great Lakes economy.

The immigration of the Halle family continued as Moses and the two brothers then sent for their sister Regina in 1850, their brother Abraham in 1853, their cousin Josephy in 1854 and their brother Loeb in 1855. A second cousin to Manuel and Moses, Joe Halle, bought the Lyceum Hall in Cleveland during the 1870s and renamed it Halle's Hall. A gathering place on the upper floor of the hall was the Excelsior Club, a private club for wealthy German-Jewish immigrants. It was the center of the family's cultural life. The hall was three stories tall with a Bavarian sweet shop on the first floor, a dinner hall and then the Excelsior Club on the top floor. The Halles frequented the hall so much that if S.P. and S.H. were searching for their father or uncle, they would stop at the club first. The Halle family also joined a local temple just south of Public Square.

When younger, both Manuel and Moses worked as clerks at the City Mill Store, a dry goods store near Public Square, with another young clerk named John D. Rockefeller. Over the next decade or so, Manuel and Rockefeller became close associates. Manuel was part of an early group of investors who pooled capital together to form Cherry Valley Oil Company, Cleveland's first oil refinery. Later, Manuel invested with William Schofield, an early competitor of Rockefeller's. Manuel and Schofield owned the only independent refinery in Cleveland that Rockefeller did not own.

Manuel had loaned Rockefeller some money that was used to acquire yet another refinery. Much of Rockefeller's early oil empire was financially supported by Manuel Halle. Manuel's wife, Augusta, found the whole oil business disgusting and (excuse the pun) unrefined, and she eventually convinced Manuel to sell all of his oil investments. Manuel then asked Moses to join him in a wholesale business that specialized in men's furnishings. In 1865, Manuel and Moses launched the M.&M. Halle Company. Their warehouse was located on Water Street (West Ninth Street) a few blocks northwest of Public Square.

A year later, a son was born to Moses and his wife, Rebecca. They named him Salmon Portland Chase Halle. In 1868, a second son was born—Samuel Horatio Halle. Rebecca unfortunately passed away in 1871. The Halle dynasty was born. Moses later married Rosa Lowentritt, and they had two daughters.

On February 6, 1891, the now grown Halle brothers, S.P. and S.H., purchased a dry goods store from the estate of Captain Thomas S. Paddock. Paddock had been a retired U.S. Army officer and had run a dry goods shop for forty-five years on Superior Street (now Avenue). The Halles paid $7,500 for the lease and inventory of the store, getting themselves into the retail game.

At this time in Cleveland history, Superior Street, both west and east of Public Square, was a great source of civic pride. The street was groomed to be the most important street for the city's commerce and trade. Trolley lines were established on Superior Street before any other avenue or road. Originally horse-drawn, the trolleys were now enhanced with cable power. Superior Street ended at the banks of the Cuyahoga River, which was teeming with ships and canalboats bringing goods, products, livestock and produce from all over the country. The Halles, though, had the misfortune of being on the "poor side" of Superior Avenue. Hower & Higbee, by now a fixture on Superior Street, had picked wisely by being on the south side of the avenue.

The new Halle's building in Playhouse Square (1910).

After buying all the Paddock inventory, the brothers opened the new Halle store to the public. It was February 7, 1891. The two men were only twenty-five (Salmon) and twenty-three (Samuel) years old. Later that first day, the first two employees (and family members), William and Eugene Halle, joined the fray. Two months later, the brothers hired the last two employees at Paddock's to join the company: Charles and Emma Ziska. The

A few stragglers at the Geranium Room Restaurant at Halle's department store, downtown Cleveland (1982).

father and daughter were cap makers and furriers and were known for their well-designed conductor caps, which were sold along the rail lines around Cleveland and Detroit all the way to Denver.

For the Superior address, the Halles were paying a premium of $300 a month in rent. Their twenty-five-foot-wide shop had five thousand square feet divided into selling space and a workroom on the ground floor, plus storage space in the basement. Despite all this space, the first year's activities were a bit disappointing. Credit and cash sales totaled $29,939.

The novice retail magnates thought it wasn't the product selection or their prices that was confining their sales growth, but rather it was the store itself. So the brothers decided that the best way to increase sales was to move to a more inviting retail storefront. They both agreed on moving the store to the Nottingham Building, which was located on Euclid Avenue at Sheriff Street (East Fourth Street). They moved the company in March 1892. Women's ready-to-wear garments appeared in the store in 1896, and it was reported that Mrs. William McKinley wore to Washington a blue serge dress and sealskin coat purchased at Halle's.[31]

By now, the Halle brothers were establishing trust with their suppliers. Louis Goldsmith, a Cleveland clothing manufacturer, worked with the brothers to supply his goods to their customers. Other prominent Cleveland clothing companies including Feiss, Printz, Skall, Sloss and Weil began courting the brothers. The Halles had a reputation for paying in cash on receipt of merchandise and thus received discounts that could be passed on to their patrons. From 1892 to 1896, sales increased by 50 percent each year. By the end of 1896, the brothers had discontinued men's furnishings, added a table for women's gloves and another for neckwear and become a specialty store for women.[32]

The new store was about to bring the brothers fame, fortune and love. A few months after moving to the Nottingham Building, S.P. took note of a young lady named Carrie Moss who would regularly shop at the store. Carrie began to notice the lavish attention S.P. would provide and became quite smitten with the young man. They were engaged in the spring of 1893 and were married on December 3 of the same year. They bought a house off Euclid Avenue and Case Street (now East Forty-Fifth Street).

Soon it would be Samuel's turn to be struck by Cupid's quiver. In 1896, Blanche Murphy arrived at the store, having resigned her sales position with Hower & Higbee Co. She was pure energy. It took a while for her to work her charms on the young bachelor, but they fell in love over time. Samuel and Blanche were married on July 12, 1901, at the Hotel Hollenden. The Hotel Hollenden was a glamorous, brawny and historic building in Cleveland. The stories of the Hollenden were legendary. Five presidents were guests. Marcus Hanna, the "President Maker and Ohio Senator," held court at the Hollenden daily, engaging in all sorts of political intrigue. It was the home of the most powerful African American entrepreneur in Cleveland, George Myers. The Hollenden did not witness history in Cleveland; the hotel was an active participant in making the history for this great city.[33] And this day proved no different. The young couple honeymooned in Maine and, upon the pair's return, moved into the Colonial Hotel on Euclid Avenue. A few months later, their home was completed on East Eighty-Ninth Street.

Despite the brothers' nuptials and growing families, the store continued to grow. It was the wonderful growth that led the brothers in 1898 to lease Shaw's old dry goods store next door, more than doubling their original space in the Nottingham. By 1905, the brothers were leasing fifty thousand square feet on six floors in the Nottingham and an adjacent building. In the basement, the company housed four wagons for deliveries and stabled six horses. The improving sales growth was giving way to thoughts of a new store. But how and when to begin looking for the next big move?

Until then, innovation was the daily mantra at the brothers' retail shop. The brothers were brash retail pioneers who helped start the nation's first advertising club and organized the Cleveland Credit Men's Co., the first cooperatively owned credit bureau. They were early and key members of the Cleveland Retail Merchants Association, an arm of the chamber of

The Georgian Room at Halle's department store, downtown Cleveland (1945).

commerce.[34] Halle's promised next-day delivery, but any guest could ask for same-day service and the store would strain its resources to make it so.

The brothers also did their best to take care of their employees. Commissions were higher at Halle's than its Cleveland counterparts. All employees received a 10 percent discount on Halle merchandise. However, one of the key employee benefits was the Employee Association. The association was founded in 1902 at Halle's as an insurance society. All employees paid into the association; dues were generally twenty-five to fifty cents a week. When an employee was sick or unable to work, the association would provide those in need with three to six dollars a week. Dues into the association also helped pay for a daily employee lunch.

But the good news gave way to a mournful reckoning. The wonderful father, Moses Halle, passed away in 1905. He was hailed as a founding father and civic hero. The Halle brothers returned to their shop, giving themselves time to lament their father's passing, more determined than ever to be successful. The Halle brothers soon overwhelmed their rented space in the Nottingham Building. It was time to move.

The once glimmering Public Square was beginning to wear down, and the city's populace and industry was shifting the city east. The mood and sentiment of Public Square and lower Euclid Avenue was beginning to turn, and not necessarily in a good way. The pride and center of Cleveland was not aging well, and soon an exodus of businesses, hotels and theaters would turn the area around Cleveland's beloved square into a ghetto full of squalor. The rapid retail shift from Public Square to places and plots on Upper Euclid was best captured by James M. Wood, author of *Halle's: Memoirs of a Family Department Store*:

> *In Cleveland, retailers huddled around Public Square in the city's increasingly shabby 50-year old retail center. John Hower had died in 1902, but his successors at The Higbee Co. were located in a five story building at Public Square and West Superior. Two blocks east of Ontario Street and Prospect Avenue, The Bailey Company had remodeled the old Burnett house so many times the original building had disappeared beneath layers of changes. E.R. Hull & Dutton, which had opened six floors on Ontario & Euclid Avenue the year the Halle Brothers bought Paddock's fur shop, had itself been bought by David May and his associates as the third store in what would become the national May Company chain.*

The May Co. and Bailey's would remain the only retailers on Public Square until Higbee's return in 1931. Others found great success moving east on Euclid Avenue. The squalor at Public Square would stay until the Van Sweringens would construct the Terminal Tower and Union Terminal complex.

Given the great growth the company was experiencing, the brothers decided it was time to place a stronger legal structure around the business. The brothers dissolved their partnership in 1906 and quickly formed a new corporation with a new name: the Halle Bros. Company. They introduced a new logo as well, using an Old English script. The script was branded on everything in the store, including wrapping paper, gift boxes, garment labels, stationery, invoices and daily newspaper advertisements.

At the time, the Halle brothers were wedged between the Arcade and other building owners unwilling to sell them land for a larger store. It was no secret the brothers were "landlocked," and some early conversations took place between them and a well-known real estate speculator, John Hartness Brown, who had, by this time, constructed a department store

Halle's new men's store on the second floor of the downtown Cleveland store (1966).

Halle's department store at Shaker Square (1953).

on the north side of Euclid Avenue near East Ninth Street. By the end of the year, upper Euclid Avenue would be transformed by the relocation of three department stores, all of which Brown wooed and none of which leased his building. During the summer, Sterling & Welch, the city's most successful furniture retailer, announced that it would lease a new store on the north side of Euclid Avenue near East Fourteenth Street. In September, the Halle brothers startled landowners by announcing plans for a new store forty blocks beyond downtown at Euclid Avenue and East Fifty-Fifth Street.[35] The Halles, of course, were bluffing.

Unfortunately for Brown, his department store had sat empty for six long years while he looked for a tenant. In 1908, he decided to try to rent the building to the Halles and began courting the brothers in earnest. Brown lied to S.H. that if the Halles would not lease Brown's building, then Higbee's might. (Higbee's was also seeking new retail space.)

John Hartness Brown started construction on his building on the north side of Euclid between the Union Trust Building and the world-famous Statler Hotel. It was 1901, and this critical development helped spur further real estate development along what was then considered Upper Euclid Avenue. The shopping district John Hartness Brown helped develop became home

Halle's department store at Summit Mall (1966).

to Cleveland's most glamorous department stores and stunning theaters. But rare is the tragic tale of John Hartness Brown.

Brown was one of Cleveland's most prominent developers. He was born in Cleveland in 1868 and early on in his career had a knack for seeing unrealized real estate development. His vision of the land south of Lake View Cemetery helped create—with another developer, Patrick Calhoun—the Euclid Heights development in 1890.[36] By 1900, Brown had controlling interests in a large tract of land in downtown Cleveland on the north side of Euclid and east of East Ninth Street. And the next year, Brown had opened ground on a new building made for a department store.

Unfortunately, Brown was soon experiencing financial problems, which led to delays in completing the building. After various lawsuits were filed against Brown, he was compelled to liquidate his interests in the land. His attorney, William H. Rice, was given control of the project and was ordered by the court to finish the construction and seek tenants. A few months after the transfer of the land, Rice was murdered. This murder stoked obvious speculation that Brown may have been involved. But the murder was never solved, and Brown left Cleveland for New York and then London, where he died in 1938.

Meanwhile, Rice's estate gave his former law partner, Frank Ginn, the right to complete the six-story structure. Many in the public called it the John Hartness Brown building, which infuriated Ginn. In 1915, Ginn hired the architectural firm George B. Post & Sons to redesign the façade of the building.[37] It maintained its six-story height but was made to look as if it were three separate buildings. To complicate matters even more, the single structure was grouped and named as if it were two buildings: the Euclid Building and the Loomis Building.

While none of the large Cleveland department stores would ever rent space in the complex, it did become home to numerous retail merchants such as B.R. Baker's (a men's clothing store), Clark's Colonial Restaurant, Wurlitzer Music Store, Stern department store and later Lane Bryant. By the 1970s, the John Hartness Brown Building was nearly empty, and in recent years, it was a significant eyesore in downtown Cleveland. It was announced in late October 2018 that Alto Partners was soon to start a $90 million project on the building. The plan for the redevelopment includes more than two hundred apartments, two hundred underground parking spaces, a rooftop lounge, a club room with a bar, a wine-tasting room with private wine lockers, an indoor golf simulator and a TV lounge.[38] As of January 2021, the redevelopment of the John Hartness Brown Building is nearly complete and is accepting applications for renters. It is a marvelous renewal of an old structure.

The Halle brothers had secretly retained Alfred Pope, president of the National Malleable Castings Co., to try to acquire land near East Fourteenth Street for a new store. The brothers were able to hide their interests until late November, when competition forced their hand. The Higbee Co. announced it would leave Public Square and lease land diagonally across the street from Pope's building for a new store.

The site Halle's selected was then occupied by single-story wood houses. There were other adjacent buildings, including the Cleveland Wheel Club, later renamed the Wyandot House Hotel, the Euclid Point Building (now a Crowne Plaza Hotel) and Winous Building. On the Huron side of the road across from the Halle development was the Benevolent and Protective Order of Elks, which had built a four-and-a-half-story building.

Pope and his business associate Harrison Whittemore purchased the site for the proposed Halle Building (or Pope Building, as it was known when first constructed) in 1905. The new Halle's store was designed by Henry Bacon, a New York city architect who later won the competition for the design of the Lincoln Memorial. The original architectural plan for the site noted a sixteen-story structure but was later reduced to a ten-story building.

To that end, Henry Bacon was an inspired choice. In fact, he received the Gold Medal of the American Institute of Architects for his design of the Lincoln Memorial. His work was greatly influenced by the Neoclassical Revival at the turn of the century. His design characteristics are displayed through the classical derived terra-cotta ornamentation enriching the façade of the building.[39] The structure also displays characteristics of the turn-of-the-century Commercial style through its distinct fenestration (the openings in the building envelop, including the installation of windows, doors and skylights), which gives the walls a skeletal appearance and provides a fairly even balance between vertical and horizontal lines. It was completed in 1910 as an eleven-story department store. Simply put, the Halle Building is an architectural gem.

The Pope Building, which abutted the Point Building, would have a brick façade clad in glazed terra cotta. In addition to the basement, there were two sub-basements (the lowest level had been intended to be a subway station). The site was full of surprises, including a large amount of quicksand. The Pope Building was to have the deepest basement in Cleveland.[40] The building offered a number of unique quirks of engineering. Built into the roof of

Walter and Samuel Halle, with a framed document (1951).

the new structure was an enormous fan that would pull in large amounts of air, which was then forced forty feet below Euclid Avenue and rinsed with a spray of water. This water was then heated or cooled, depending on the season, and pumped back into the store and expelled as exhaust every twenty minutes. Also, the fifth floor held the fur storage vault, which had been placed behind a door decorated as though it were an entrance to an Egyptian tomb.

On November 28, 1908, the Halle Bros. Department Store signed a long-term lease for the entire Pope Building. It doubled the space from Halle's current location near the Grand Arcade. The final cost of construction was nearly $1.5 million. The Pope Building opened to the public in February 1910.

The impetus that helped to spur the relocation and development of the city's major business district to Upper Euclid Avenue in the early 1900s is widely credited to the Halle Building. Others soon found success in the Upper Euclid district, including Higbee's, Sterling Welch and W.B. Davis department stores. So did a half dozen theaters and office buildings that clustered about Halle's. They eventually formed a splendid new entertainment district—Playhouse Square—that shifted downtown Cleveland's center of gravity twelve blocks east from Public Square.[41]

The Nottingham Building store closed for business on a late Saturday in February 1910, and all the remaining inventory had to be packed and shipped to the new store. All day Sunday, old stock and new merchandise that had been shipped directly to the new store was sorted, marked and arranged by more than five hundred employees, more than three hundred of whom were new. The Nottingham Building was used way beyond its means, and at the end, Halle's had occupied nearly 50,000 square feet in the building. The new store would be almost three times as large, offering 140,000 square feet of retail nirvana. Sales surpassed $1 million for the first time in the company's history.

Now there would be three major nodes of development in downtown Cleveland: Public Square, a new retail center at East Fourteenth Street and a major new civic center that would stretch north six blocks from East Superior Avenue near the Arcade to a bluff overlooking Lake Erie. The Pope Building was the beginning of new construction along Euclid Avenue. The Swetland Building (1010 Euclid) was added in 1910, and the Cleveland Athletic Club building was finished in 1911.

The location proved to be quite central. Sales at Halle's continued to increase, dramatically. At the end of 1911, the brothers were thrilled to note that sales were in excess of $2 million. Sales had doubled since moving to the Pope Building.

By 1912, Pope agreed to build an addition for the Halle's store. A new ten-story addition was added to the west of the original structure.

Halle's special occasion shop (1967).

The addition was a perfect copy of the original building. When finished and opened to the public in November 1914, the new space increased the total square footage to 425,0000. This larger floor plan for the store allowed Halle's to now offer candy, furniture and men's clothing. The most dramatic change occurred on the main floor with the installation of a stunning marble staircase paired with bronze lightoliers that led to a mezzanine. The mezzanine was stocked full of merchandise and included an information desk where customers could write letters or purchase tickets to plays or concerts, several public telephones, a kiosk to drop off dry cleaning and a post office. Underneath the mezzanine was a new Men's Row, which included four shops that had separate entrances on an arcade running between Euclid Avenue and Huron Road.

A new seventy-five-seat men's lunchroom was included on the seventh floor, along with two tearooms, one done up in American Colonial style and the other in a Japanese style. While moms enjoyed their tea, the children were welcome to join the fun at the Halle's playground. Here, kids could enjoy a sandbox, a house and other playground equipment. There was a golf green as well. The roof house had glass walls and ceilings and contained a lunchroom, men's smoking room and women's lounge, all for the exclusive use of employees. Beneath the street, the subway entrance was still unused, despite Cleveland's city manager William Hopkins promising imminent construction of a high-speed subway under Euclid.

In 1916, the Halle Bros. Company celebrated its twenty-fifth anniversary. It was the beginning of a tradition of honoring any employee who held twenty-five years of service at Halle Bros. The company picnic that year was held at HalleFarm near Kirtland, Ohio. S.H. had acquired 285 acres of land that had a log cabin and a cattle barn.[42] HalleFarm was the grand getaway for the entire Halle family, but it was S.H. who really immersed himself in the Kirtland escape.

There was a summer house on the grounds, as well as a visitors' cottage, a horse stable, a vineyard, a rose garden, a swimming pool, tennis courts and, if necessary, an airstrip. S.H. had also built a suspension bridge over a small gorge and connected the summer house to the cottage. The gorge was known as Penitentiary Gulch.[43]

It was a working farm as well, as the Halles hired for many years the Burnett family to live and work on the grounds year round. The Halle family would host parties, community celebrations and important visitors at HalleFarm every summer. S.H. continued to visit the summer home until his death in 1954. After his death, his children inherited the farm. The Cleveland Metroparks purchased the farm in 1975. People can tour the grounds today.

Sales at Halle's at the end of 1918 grew to $3.7 million. The Halle brothers' dream of building a real American department store was becoming true. But soon, it became Samuel's responsibility, as Salmon P.

Halle's Annex Building is the large white building in the foreground, while the Halle's department store is the white structure in the background (1953).

Halle resigned from the company. S.P. had wanted to retire once he turned fifty years old. Four years past his personal deadline, S.P. presented S.H. with a confidential, eight-page memorandum detailing how and when he was to retire. S.H. worked with the board to make S.P.'s desires happen in quick order.

S.P. then devoted himself to philanthropies and private interests. And in 1921, his brother Samuel succeeded him as president. Samuel bought Salmon out for $1 million in Halle Bros. Company preferred stock, paying out a healthy 8 percent annual interest.

Many important expansions were made during Samuel's regime. To begin with, in 1922 he purchased the Elks Club Building on Huron Road to the west, providing expansion opportunities such as the Halle Annex. When Samuel decided in 1924 to construct an annex to the company's fourteen-year-old Euclid Avenue department store, it was clear that it should match the original building. The store's fortunes continued to grow, and by the end of 1924, the company employed nearly 1,500 people.

View of Euclid Avenue and Huron Avenue intersections with Halle's in the background. Note the large painted Halle's sign on the building (1936).

Halle Bros. Company was now the second-largest department store in Cleveland, which was now the nation's fifth-largest city. Only May Company could claim to exceed Halle in terms of revenue. At the end of 1925, sales at Halle had exceeded $14 million.

The store's extraordinary financial health attracted the interest of two reclusive bachelor brothers, Orris Paxton and Mantis James Van Sweringen. The Vans were building a giant complex on the southeast corner of Public Square that was to include a new union depot, an office tower and a new department store linked above and below ground with the existing Hotel Cleveland.

The Vans heavily pursued S.H., trying to convince him to become the keystone of a revitalized retail center at Public Square. They knew he needed more space. Menswear and home furnishings were, indeed, cramped. The receiving docks were inadequate. S.H. knew this, of course, and didn't need the Vans reminding him of the building's shortcomings. Instead of joining the Vans, S.H. decided it was the right time to expand across Huron Road. Walker & Weeks, Cleveland architects extraordinaire, were retained soon thereafter.

Walker & Week's plans for the Halle Annex were unveiled in March 1926. The distinguishing details of Bacon's elegant design were repeated on the six-story Huron-Prospect Building—crisp, precise terra-cotta detail; graceful segmental arches at the second story, with their simulated voussoirs (a wedge-shaped or tapered stone used to construct an arch); and boldly molded garlands above the third story.

In addition, the Halles proposed to link the two structures across Huron Road with a two-level bridge at the fourth and fifth floors. The buildings were ninety feet apart, and the bridge would span the street fifty-five feet above the pavement. Walker & Weeks' design shows a light, fanciful arch of Venetian inspiration, topped by an imposing bronze clock. It is not unlikely that they referred to the similar bridge at Wanamaker's store in Philadelphia.

However, neighboring property owners objected to the bridge and won a court injunction against the Halle Bros. Company. (There were rumors that

Lucille Ball at Halle's, downtown Cleveland (1956).

the Van Sweringen brothers were the silent voices behind the injunction.) Instead, the only link between the two buildings was the underground tunnel, thus creating a continuous 450-foot-long sales aisle between Euclid and Prospect Avenue. Deftly hidden inside the tunnel's walls were miles of telephone lines, executive call systems and vacuum tubes that provided almost instantaneous communication between far-flung departments of the ever-expanding Halle retail complex in downtown.

The Halle Bros. Company opened its new $5 million, six-story Huron-Prospect Building on May 31, 1927. At this time, Huron Road was a district of old but imposing residences, and the Halle store influenced improvements of the area. This new addition more than doubled the store's retail space. The contractor on the project was John Gill & Sons. S.H. had decided that the entire first floor of the new addition would be an exclusive men's store. Its new dark mahogany paneling and carved marble details were reminiscent of a rich man's private club. Behind the elevator walls on the first floor was the club's inner sanctum, a six-chair barbershop. Nothing like this had been built in Cleveland before, and it was a tremendous success.

On the fifth floor of Halle's new Huron building was a complete English manor home, re-created from historical models. The store's artists and craftsmen had copied three-hundred-year-old wooden panels for the manor's entry. A library built with stone fireplaces, polished floors, stained-glass windows and hung draperies were included in this magnificent re-creation. On the roof of the new building, there were large arrows providing pilots in airplanes navigational support to find the Cleveland airport.

Also, in 1927 the store took receipt of twenty-two White Motor Company trucks manufactured in Cleveland and dismissed its older fleet of Baker electric cars. The trucks added speed and capacity for the store's daily deliveries to customers' homes.

On a more personal note, S.P., now retired, hired John William Cresswell Corbusier to design his new home in Shaker Heights. The year was 1927, and S.P. had just acquired some land on Park Drive. Corbusier was a well-known architect more known for his design of churches than of homes. Over his career, Corbusier designed thirty churches, eleven of which are in the northeast Ohio area. Surprisingly, all of the churches remain standing, including the Church of the Covenant, located in University Heights, and the Church of the Savior, in Cleveland Heights.

Corbusier constructed a dynamic, thoughtful and expressive home for S.P. Halle's family. The home is situated on four grassy, green acres and was built in a French Renaissance style. The home has more than fifteen thousand square feet of living space. The mansion features glass entrances, gable dormers with spiral scroll ornaments, massive cornerstones and beautiful voussoirs. The construction took two long years to complete. The family loved the home and lived there until 1965, when Halle's widow, Carrie, finally passed away. The family sold the home as part of Carrie's estate.[44] The home was designated a Shaker Heights landmark in 1976.

For many years, Halle had employed a number of agents who would travel to small towns in northern Ohio and western Pennsylvania and sell a select amount of department store goods. The agents would take up residence in a local hotel and turn the room into an attractive setting for the display of women's fashion. They ladies would order the clothing, and it would later be sent to them in the mail.

S.H. felt it might prove financially prudent to open small Halle Bros. stores in five cities that were sitting on interurban routes. The interurban, especially in the United States, was a valuable cultural institution. Most roads and town streets were unpaved, and transportation was by horse-drawn carriages and carts. By the turn of the century, interurbans radiated out of Cleveland to Akron, Canton, Painesville, Lorain, Elyria, Oberlin, Medina and even the remote reaches of rural Geauga Country. Within three years, they would reach as far as Toledo and Wooster.[45]

The interurban provided vital transportation links between the city and countryside. In 1915, 15,500 miles (24,900 kilometers) of interurban railways were operating in the United States. For a time, interurban railways were the fifth-largest industry in the United States.[46] Given the rapid acceptance of the automobile, the interurbans started to lose a large number of customers. By 1930, most interurbans were gone, with few surviving into the 1950s. But for a period of time, these small rail lines were quite promising and connected many small cities and towns with larger cities. In 1927, Halle's started to review sites for its new branch stores to be located in Erie and New Castle, Pennsylvania, and the small cities of Canton, Warren and Mansfield in Ohio.

A special relationship was developed during the interurban store expansion between Halle's and the world-famous Cleveland-based architectural firm of Walker & Weeks. The architectural firm designed the branch stores in Canton and Warren, Ohio, during 1928–29. S.H. Halle called on the firm again twenty years later. At first it was for the proposed extension to the original building to the angled point

Halle's downtown Christmas display window (1979).

of Huron Road and Euclid Avenue. Instead, having decided that the triangular plan was uneconomical, the company built a west wing facing on Huron and bridging East Twelfth Street to connect with the Euclid Avenue building, added three stories to the original 1910 building and constructed a service building on Prospect next to the Huron-Prospect Building.[47]

Even in later years, after a generation of the Great Depression, war and modernism, all of these additions once again displayed the same decorative details as the original Halle building. In fact, Samuel Halle served as an honorary pallbearer for the architect Frank Ray Walker of Walker & Weeks in 1949.

At the end of 1929, Halle's had earned $20 million in revenue. Then the Great Depression hit. Sales were down by 12 percent in 1930. In 1931, sales declined another 17 percent. The store was blessed with a $4 million cash surplus on its balance sheet, courtesy of the rigid financial acumen of S.H. Halle. Cuts had to be made nonetheless; the financial perils of the Depression were too daunting for any enterprise, much less a retail store.

By 1932, most of the workers who had not been let go worked at most three days a week. Commissioned salespeople were paid their weekly guaranteed draws even though their commissions failed to cover their expenses. S.H. Halle did his best to keep his company and his employees together. The only assets many employees had in their possession was their Savings Bureau Account (which did not survive the Depression) through the store and their $1,000 life insurance policy, which Halle's purchased on behalf of the employee after their first year at the store.

In 1930, Halle's introduced a new College Shop on the fourth floor of the Euclid Avenue building. This was in response to more of its customers sending their kids to college, even if in desperate times. The year 1932 brought out the worst financial period for Halle's. Sales that year plummeted 25 percent from the previous year. Sales were now only $11 million, a bit more than half of what revenue was in 1929. It was looking rather grim. Despite the desperate times, Halle's announced a new renovation project for the Elks building on Huron Avenue in 1933. The building was prepped for a number of charitable and nonprofit organizations that could not afford rent in the big city. Even with dwindling sales, Halle's was more interested in helping others.

The big news in 1933, both locally and nationally, was the absolute and final collapse of the Van Sweringen brothers' vast business empire. It was a jolting collapse for the publicly shy duo. Many investors in Cleveland, both institutional and individual, were left with worthless shares. Halle's could not navigate the choppy financial waters either, and the decision was made in 1934 to close the Mansfield, Ohio and New Castle, Pennsylvania stores.

In 1935, the Higbee Company filed for bankruptcy protection. The announcement of the filing came as a surprise to many, with the one possible exception of the controller of Higbee's, who was facing payroll being due on the very day of the announcement. The Cleveland banks would not agree to provide cash to cover Higbee's payroll. Executives of Higbee's reluctantly called Halle's to see if they might be able to help. It was an easy decision. Halle's had $40,000 on hand and immediately couriered it over to Higbee's, and a short-term loan was agreed to. Higbee's employees were paid.

Around this time, Walter Halle, the son of S.H., began taking more responsibility at the department store chain. He was responsible for the fashionable modernization of the third and fourth floors of the Euclid Avenue building during 1935 and 1936. In 1938, S.H. celebrated his seventieth birthday, and he was looking to retire. He started to plan for his ultimate gift to the employees who made Halle's a magical place.

On his seventy-second birthday in 1941, S.H. was quietly huddled with his son Walter and a number of bankers inside a large conference room at the Cleveland Trust building on the corner of Euclid Avenue and East Ninth. It was during this meeting that S.H. gave the bankers a list of 886 employees who had worked at the store for more than a year. And each one of them was about to receive the golden ticket—shares of Halle's stock. One share each. S.H. then handed the flabbergasted bankers another list of 882 individuals who had worked diligently at the store for more than five years. They were to receive three shares. And finally, he handed over to the incredulous bankers a final list of 349 employees who had worked more than fifteen years. Each of them received five shares. These were not newly issued shares but rather stock from S.H.'s personal holdings. Both S.H. and Walter were beaming.

S.H. had planned to leave by the end of 1941. Walter had now been at the store for thirteen years, and S.H. felt his son was ready to grow the fortunes of the store. That summer, however, Walter was selected in the Selective Service draft. He joined the Air Transport Command and was sent to Wright Patterson Air Force base in Dayton, Ohio.

After World War II, Halle's was ready for a new expansion on its current facility. By 1945, the company had already acquired the Elks building (1051 Huron Road) and the Wyandot Building (1103 Huron Road) as part of a planned $10 million expansion. Back in 1944, Halle's had assumed a lease for the triangular plot next to the east wall of the original building. And before S.H.'s retirement, he had retained Walker & Weeks to design a building for that space. (Today, this space is filled by the Crowne Plaza Hotel at Playhouse Square.) The unveiled design, if it had been built, would have been a monumental architectural centerpiece for Halle's. Walter and others at Halle's thought the design was too narrow for retail space and opted out.

Walter Halle was elected president of Halle's on April 11, 1946. His father assumed the chairman of the board title. Jay Iglauer, who worked with the Halle family for many years at the store, became executive vice president and treasurer. As part of the company's expansion program, executives were planning a large branch store to be built on Shaker Boulevard on Shaker Square. Plans were also underway for an eleven-story building to replace the Halle Annex.

But Walter was the perfect person to operate the business in the new world order after World War II. When Walter took over as president, telephone sales had doubled, and the switchboard was now open twenty-four hours a day. The catalogue department was filling orders from seven hundred letters and two thousand phone calls a day. People weren't coming into the store as they once used to but still desired that Halle style and prestige.

The downtown building did not get attention until 1947. The plans for the downtown building were extraordinary. A new addition to the Euclid building was planned and would be twelve stories. The roof of the two earlier buildings was removed. New elevators and escalators were installed. On Prospect Avenue, east of the twenty-year-old Huron-Prospect Building, a new structure was being built. At six stories high, it offered only one selling floor. The rest of the space was for service workers. All construction was completed by the fall of 1949.

Halle's personnel examining a fancy tablecloth (1939).

Wall mural of ancient Minoans at Halle's downtown store. It was painted by Daniel Rasmussen on five walls up to fourteen feet high in Halle's tearoom.

A total of 100,000 square feet of retail space was added. Two new floors were added, as well as a fifteen-room health clinic, hospital and dental center on the eleventh floor. The twelfth floor held the air conditioning and much of the new mechanicals. The western portion of the twelfth floor housed the Halle's employee lounge, which had a staircase that led to the roof where employees could enjoy a rooftop garden.

By the time Walter had assumed operating control of the business, May Company was the largest department store by revenue. Halle's was second, Higbee's third and Bailey's a distant fourth. Higbee's had rallied after emerging from bankruptcy and under the leadership of John Murphy. Murphy's clever decision to join the Associated Merchandising Corp. (a buying cooperative out of New York) aided Higbee's profitability. Nevertheless, at the end of 1946, Halle's sales were $38 million—a record year.

The suburbs were the next frontier for Halle's. A Cleveland Heights store was opened in 1947. Walter and his team remodeled an existing building on the corner of Fairmount and Cedar Roads. Two years later,

Halle's built a new store on Shaker Square, trying its best to steal some of Higbee's Shaker customers. In 1951, a second Cleveland Heights store was opened at Cedar Center. Not even a year later, Halle's opened a store outside of Erie, Pennsylvania. And finally, in 1954, a gleaming new Halle's store was opened at Westgate Shopping Mall in Fairview Park.

Walter believed he was solving the new retail challenges of the post–World War II environment. His aggressive expansion in both downtown Cleveland and in various suburbs had brought on significant debt to the company. His strategy, while not hotly contested by executives and employees, was debated and questioned, most notably by Walter's own family, especially his sisters Margaret (married to Francis Sherwin), Jane (married to George Crile Jr.), Ann (married to Robert Little) and Kay. The sisters were focused on the look and feel of the downtown store and were less concerned about expansion.

Nevertheless, Walter took a creative approach to an engaging customer experience. He created the 1228 Club, one of the first men's shopping services. Many of Cleveland's elite lusted after Walter's annual invitation to attend a special VIP cocktail reception, a fashion show and then comradery until the wee hours of the morn. Only one thousand businessmen in the city received the invite—a golden ticket.

Walter was also ahead of his time in sensing the fashion trends of America. He was able to convince a struggling Estee Lauder to sell her cosmetics line exclusively at Halle's. He did the same for Bill Blass. Despite all of Walter's retail flair, sales were not growing as fast as at other local department store chains. By the end of 1950, Halle's was in third place in revenue behind May Company and Higbee's.

Sad news came to the entire Halle family on August 11, 1954. S.H. passed away, leaving an amazing legacy. Walter and his wife, Helen, were moments from boarding a luxury ocean liner for a well-earned cruise when they received the phone call. S.H. had died in his sleep at his beloved home on Harcourt Drive. On August 13, over one thousand people crowded into the auditorium in the west wing of the department store to bereave and celebrate the late retail icon. Brit Hadden and Henry Luce, the publishers of *Time* magazine, listed him as the last member of a celebrated group of retail giants—Wanamaker, Bamberger, David May and Marshall Field. (Both Hadden and Luce spent time with Halle at his home on Harcourt Drive while the magazine was headquartered in Cleveland for a short period.)

In 1955, management decided to move all the merchandise out of the Huron-Prospect Building into the west wing of the Euclid Building. The

Millinery department and furs at Halle's downtown store (1937).

first three floors in the Huron space were used for parking. Some new outside tenants took space in a couple of floors, while shipping and storage were now on the fourth through sixth floors. To improve a shrinking shopping population for the downtown store, Halle's purchased a fleet of buses from the Cleveland Transit System to provide free transportation from Public Square to the store on Euclid.

A long-planned, and completely financed, subway system was announced in 1953 with a planned stop at the Halle Building. County engineer Albert Porter, however, thought it was a waste of time and money and allowed the bond issue to expire. The subway was never built. The original plan for the subway was established by the Van Sweringen brothers during the development of Terminal Tower and the attached Union Station. The brothers thought a subway should eventually be built from the Union Station under Huron Road, then connect to Euclid at East Fourteenth under Halle's and then continue under Euclid Avenue all the way to University Circle. There were architectural designs of the

Halle storefront that clearly show a subway entrance on the corner of Euclid Avenue and East Fourteenth. What could have been.

Mr. Jingeling, the "Keeper of the Keys," is fondly remembered by several generations of Clevelanders. He was Santa's most important helper who lived in the Treasure House of Toys on the store's iconic seventh floor. Mr. Jingeling was created in 1956 by Chicago ad agent Frank Jacobi for the purpose of helping to boost Christmas sales at Halle's. Mr. Jingeling was such a hit at Halle's that a local children's TV program, *Captain Penny*, picked him up as a regular character. The story goes that Mr. Jingeling was the Keeper of the Keys to Santa's workshop. The character, which was portrayed as a lovable, white-bearded elf in a fur-lined green suit, has been played by five actors since then, perhaps most notably by Earl W. Keyes, a local actor who bought the rights to Mr. Jingeling after Halle's and later Higbee's went out of business.[48]

Playhouse Square was going through some challenging times in the 1960s. A new Bonwit Teller had opened in the old Linder department store space. But many buildings and theaters in the area were closing. To help improve the Playhouse Square area, Halle's became a stockholder in the 918 Corporation. The organization had crafted a plan to acquire a significant number of properties west of the Huron-Prospect Building and then construct a new office tower, to be called the Halle Towers, and a hotel.

Walter's son Chisholm Halle (or Chis, as everyone called him) joined the board in 1961 and was beginning to take on more responsibility for the day-to-day activities of the company. Walter experienced a continued illness from late 1965 to 1966. Eventually, he agreed to move to the chairmanship position while Chis became president of the company.

New president, new outlook, new way of doing business. Chis decided early on in his tenure to lessen the expenditure in newspaper advertisements and focused the bulk of the advertising budget into TV and radio ads. He was more apt to fill an open position at Halle's by skill rather than seniority, which had become a Halle's tradition. He took great interest in modernizing displays, redecorating the downtown store, and took a huge risk in changing the traditional Halle's Old English script for a more modern font. Chis also saved many of the theaters in Playhouse Square. He formed the Cleveland Downtown Properties, Inc. with two other real estate developers and bought two theaters and an office building. It was the beginning of a movement to save the theaters.

What was becoming evident was that Halle lacked the financial resources that the May Company immediately had at its disposal. Chis strongly

Stage display of ladies' fashion coasts at Halle's downtown store (1937).

Cars parked in front of Halle's at Cedar Center (1950).

desired to keep an aggressive suburban expansion moving forward. He wanted to add new dimensions to the downtown store and was keenly aware of the need of new wholesale strategy. Halle's could not compete with Higbee's on wholesale pricing because Higbee's was part of the Associated Merchandise Corporation (AMC). AMC was based out of New York and bought for numerous regional department stores, thus gaining a wholesale pricing edge.

Walter felt it was time to perhaps begin some conversations with other national chains and see if any were interested in acquiring Halle's. Chis was a bit more reluctant but understood the reality; if he wanted to expand, he needed the capital to do so. So in the summer of 1970, Walter and Chis traveled to Chicago to meet with the executive team of Marshall Field & Company. Chis finally signed the merger agreement between Halle's and Field's that would provide the terms of the merger. Essentially, Halle stockholders would exchange their shares for Field's stock, in effect merging the nine Halle stores in Ohio and Pennsylvania into the Field's operation for $13 million.

Halle's revenue at the end of 1970 was $70 million. Was the company worth more than $13 million in Marshall Field & Company stock? A case could be made that Halle's stock was worth considerably more. In fact, after the first year of operating within the Field's operations, Halle's accounted for more than a third of Field's total revenue of $200 million.

But the signs of a plagued marriage were seen soon after the ink dried on the merger agreement. In early 1971, the executives at Marshall Field's instructed Chis to eliminate twenty-three middle managers and executives—a curious request since it was reported that Field's would be a "hands-off" owner. It was an act that simply did not happen at Halle's. The store took care of its own. A few months later, Walter was notified that he would not be sitting on Field's board of directors, a position that he was promised but went, instead, to a Chicago-based executive who was in the copier business. Walter immediately resigned his position as chairman of Halle's.

Walter Halle died in January 1972, a sad day for the entire Halle's family. He was a wonderful family man, devoted husband and father. He was groomed to be a retail scion of a particular age and time, and when the macro events of the retail trade changed, his family did not have the financial depth to take full advantage of the shift to suburbia. He was a civically minded soul, a rare haberdasher and a retail icon. His loss hit the Halle family hard. And perhaps the loss hit the employees and shoppers at Halle's even harder.

The pressure continued on the family from their Chicago masters. In March 1972, Field's executives demanded that Halle relinquish its real estate holdings in Playhouse Square. This action leaves one to wonder how Halle's investments and new office construction would have changed Playhouse Square for the better a good generation before the Playhouse Square renaissance. In 1973, Chis Halle resigned as president of Halle's, thus ending a long, unbroken chain of the family running the department store. Chis eventually opened Chisholm Halle's, a boutique retail store featuring upscale men's and women's clothing.

For Halle's, the much-vaunted buying power and working capital of Field's never materialized to help support suburban expansion and downtown revitalization projects. Field's coveted Halle's name and revenue and nothing else. In the Cleveland retail race with able competitors like Higbee's and May Company, Halle's needed sales expansion, not cost cutting. Halle's required new capital to compete. Field's was ready to let the chain starve. Field's did help introduce new medium-priced products, which seemed to confuse Halle's shoppers and not help the profitability of the stores.

Life on Euclid Avenue in front of Halle Bros. (1963).

Rumors began to spread in early 1979 that executives in Chicago were shopping Halle's to Macy's or Lazarus out of Columbus. Those rumors never materialized. Instead, in that same year, Field's acquired the Union Store department chain in Columbus, Ohio, and turned its locations into Halle stores. Higbee's approached Marshall Field executives in 1980 to acquire the Halle's brand but was turned down.[49]

It wasn't until November 1981 that Field's announced that it had sold the company. All fifteen stores and the great downtown Halle complex were sold to Jerome Schottenstein. It was unfortunately a deal with the devil. Schottenstein was a corporate raider of the worst kind and had acquired other retail chains—Korvettes and W.T. Grant—only to liquidate the stores and shutter the brands.

Schottenstein took the unusual steps of taking out full-page ads in Cleveland's daily newspapers to inform Halle's customers that he was going to run Halle's like a real business and turn the stores around. On January 18, 1982, Chis Halle unexpectedly passed away. His was a life fully lived but cut too short. He was forty-eight years old. His death sent shockwaves through the Cleveland community and especially among Halle's employees. Not two weeks later, Schottenstein announced that he was going to close all the Halle's stores and liquidate their merchandise. The Halle closeout sale took place one day short of the company's ninety-first anniversary.

Soon after Halle's closed in 1982, the building was slated to be redeveloped into offices. Forest City Enterprises acquired 50 percent of the building, with Schottenstein owning the other half. This redevelopment included tearing down part of the Point Building on Euclid and redirecting Huron Street to abruptly turn north at Euclid Avenue. A hotel was announced to be built on the site of the Point Building in 1987. In 1993, the Wyndham Hotel at Playhouse Square was opened to the public. It now operates as a Crowne Plaza.

K&D acquired the Halle Building and the parking garage across the street for $20 million in 2014, after studying what real estate concept would work for the site. Later, it was announced that floors six through ten of the Halle Building were going to be rebuilt as apartments, branded the Residences at Halle. Amenities for residents include a fitness center and parking in the Huron Road garage. The apartments opened in the late summer of 2018.

THE STORE

The Halle Building is a magnificent piece of architecture that adds a certain gravitas to Euclid Avenue. The various architects who worked on the building alone would merit scholarly interest. Better yet, it offers Cleveland a grand sense of pride. The gleaming white terra cotta–clad building exudes confidence and luxury. While not the center of Cleveland's retail universe anymore, it is still visual evidence of the city's grand and glamorous past.

The building has become iconic in the entertainment industry. In the late 1990s, the Halle building was set as the fictional Winfred-Louder store on *The Drew Carey Show*. A scene for the *Spider Man 3* movie was filmed in front of the Halle building. Simply put, it is a gorgeous, well-designed building that merits new life, which it has as luxury apartments. The following section details the retail floors when Halle's was at its zenith as a retail power in the Sixth City.

Basement

Halle's Basement Store

First Floor

Fine Jewelry • Costume Jewelry • Fine Watches • Handbags • Personal Leather Goods • Gloves • Belts • Hosiery • Slipper Bar • Scarves • Fashion Accessories • Hat Bar • Blouses • Sweaters • Career Sportswear • Sandpiper Shop • Rain Shop • Notions • Stationery • Adult Game Shop • Candy Shop • The Eye Store • Discovery Shop • Beauty Worlds Fragrances • Cosmetics • Men's Bar • Store for Men's Accessories • Men's Grooming World • Men's Furnishings • Men's Sportswear

Mezzanine

Wine Shop • Mezzanine Café • Gift Wrapping Service • Repair Service • 1228 Club • Store for Men • Land Sea Air Travel

Second Floor

Casual Shoes • Career Shoes • Shoe Salon • Contemporary Shoes • Millinery • Wig Salon • Christmas Center • Candle Shop • Store for Men • Men's Clothing • Designer Showcase • Kirtland Shop • Men's Sportswear • His Place • Men's Shoes • Men's Hats • The Young Men's Shop • Student Shop

Third Floor
Misses' Dresses • Misses' Coats • Young Idea Shop • Dress Salon • Coat Salon • Suit Salon • Studio III • Inner Circle • The Specialty Shop • Fur Salon • YSL/Rive Gauche Boutique • Bridal Salon • Young Designer Shop • Designer Sportswear

Fourth Floor
Career Shop • Career Coats • Town and Travel Shop • Everyday Dresses • Uniforms • Sportswear • Super Sport • Beach Shop • Country Clothes • Studio IV • Here and Now • Women's Shop • Junior Shop • Junior Dresses • Junior Sportswear • Junior Coats

Fifth Floor
Intimate Apparel • Daytime Lingerie • Foundations • Body Shoppe • Sleepwear • Loungewear • Intimate Boutique • Loungewear • Junior Intimate Apparel • Maternity Shop • Children's World Infants' Wear • Toddlers • Boys' Wear • Tiny Finery • Girls' Wear • Accessories • Young Shoes • Carousel Shop for Junior High Girls

Sixth Floor
Art Needlework • Fashion Fabrics • Sewing Machines • Curtains and Draperies • Slipcovers • Cushions • Pillow Shop • Floor Coverings • Beauty Salon

Seventh Floor
China • Wedgwood Studio • Rosenthal Studio • Fine Artwares • Silver • Glassware • Crystal • Steuben Glass Room • Bridal Registry • Casual Living • Decorative Accessories • Linens and Domestics • Toy Shop • Seventh Floor Lounge

Eighth Floor
Housewares • Gourmet Galleries • Major Appliances • Garden Shop • Home Improvements • Luggage • Sporting Goods • Ski Chalet • Pro Shop • Camera and Optics • TV Center • Stereo Center • Records • Piano Salon • Organ Salon • Bedroom Furniture • Dining Room Furniture • Living Room Furniture • Mattresses • Occasional Furniture • Interior Design Service • Ski Chalet

Ninth Floor
The Book Shop • Lamps • Picture Gallery • Mirrors • Cloud 9 Shop • Sleep Shop • Summer Furniture • Contemporary Furniture • The Geranium Room • The Patio Room • Portrait Studio

Tenth Floor
Upholstered Furniture • Traditional Furniture • Furniture Gallery • Crossroads Market • Model Rooms • The Hunting Valley Shop • Interior Design Studio • Executive Gifts

Eleventh Floor
Cashier • Credit Office • Personnel Office • Employees' Lounge

THE CHARACTERS

Manuel and Moses Halle

Both Manuel and Moses Halle were immigrants from Bavaria who made their fortunes as wholesalers in Cleveland, Ohio. Moses was the father to both Salmon P. Halle and Samuel H. Halle. Moses made his way to Cleveland in 1848, joining his brother Manuel.

Manuel had established a profitable partnership with William C. Schofield, one of Big Oil's early pioneers and the protagonist to John D. Rockefeller. The partnership was dissolved in 1865, and Manuel used the proceeds to start a wholesaling business with his younger brother. The business was known as M. Halle & Company, and they were purveyors of men's furnishings. Their warehouse was located on Water Street, four blocks northwest of Public Square.[50]

The wholesale company prospered for both men and eventually sold out to other family members. Both men retired at the age of fifty and placed all of their active business interests—banking and real estate holdings—into M.&M. Halle Company. Moses became a director of his son's retail business. Both men were members of the Excelsior Club, a private enclave for wealthy, first-generation German-Jewish immigrants.

Manuel was born on February 11, 1832. He married Augusta Weil in 1863, and they had five children: Ida, Nora, William, Delia and Eugene. He passed away on November 24, 1932. Moses was born in 1834 and died on December 4, 1905. He was married to Rebecca Weil, Augusta's sister, and had sons Salmon and Samuel. After Rebecca's death, Moses married Rosa Lowentritt in 1874 and had two daughters, Jessie and Minnie.[51]

Salmon Portland Chase Halle

S.P. was born in Cleveland as the firstborn to Rebecca and Moses Halle. He attended the great Cleveland public schools of the time with his younger brother Samuel. On December 3, 1893, Salmon married Carrie Moss. They had two children, a daughter named Marion and a son named Portland. The family lived in a French-style villa in Shaker Heights that was built by John William Creswell Corbusier, a Cleveland-based architect better known for the thirty churches he helped design and build.

Salmon retired from Halle's Bros. in 1921 after being bought out by his brother. He maintained an office in the Hanna Building for years while engaging in his philanthropic work. He was a key figure in the Cleveland

Halle's delivery van makes a special delivery to a happy customer (1930).

The Shaker Square Halle's branch store (year not listed). *Courtesy of Wetzler's Photography.*

Advertising Club, the Community Fund and the Jewish Welfare Federation and a financial contributor to the Mount Sinai Medical Center. Salmon also donated works of art to the Cleveland Museum of Art.[52] While still active in the business, Salmon was a director at the Mutual Building and Loan Company and the Service Recorder Company. He passed away on September 13, 1949.

Samuel Horatio Halle

S.H. was born to Moses Halle and Rebecca Weil in 1868. His family was one of the most powerful Jewish families in Cleveland. Both his father and uncle were power brokers in banking, industry, wholesaling and real estate. He married Blanche Murphy, and they had five children: Katherine, Walter, Margaret, Jane and Ann.

During World War I, S.H. volunteered for military service and was commissioned a major. He entered into the Quartermaster Corps and was sent to Kansas City in August 1917. A few weeks later, he was transferred to Washington, D.C., at the request of one of the most powerful men in Cleveland and D.C., Newton Baker. S.H. resigned his commission in early 1918 and returned to the growing Halle Bros. department store.

S.H.'s wife, Blanche, died in late 1951. He was never quite the same after her passing. He visited the store daily after retiring. He passed away on August 11, 1954, in his sleep at the family home on Harcourt Drive. During his funeral, nearly 1,100 people crowded into the Halle auditorium. He was praised as a retail icon and great family man. It was his gift of his own personal equity interests in the Halle Bros. Company to his employees that resonated for generations.

Time magazine listed S.H. as the last survivor of a group of retailing giants that included John Wanamaker, Louis Bamberger, David May and Marshall Field. He was widely praised as a merchant, philanthropist and patron of the arts. Editor of the *Cleveland Press* Louis Seltzer wrote in an editorial about S.H. that "Cleveland had grown spiritually, civically, industrially, culturally because of Sam Halle, for no good thing for Cleveland has ever wanted for his help."[53]

After his passing, his children sold the beloved Halle red brick Georgian house on the corner of Harcourt Drive and Cedar Road. Family friend and *Cleveland Press* columnist Winsor French drearily noted the loss of man and home:

> *By the time I reached it last Friday the frantic mobs, for the most part, had dispersed. The house itself had that somewhat forlorn, resigned look that sometimes comes to the very ill when they only wish everyone would go away and leave them alone to their aches and pains. The sales people looked tired and harried. The furnishings, pictures, and odd pieces of bric-a-brac seemed strangely unfamiliar and the people pawing over them appeared to be lost and at loose ends, as if they didn't know what on earth they were looking for. But they came and went, while a bored young detective standing at the door asked people to douse their cigarettes.*[54]

Walter Halle

Walter passed away at his home in Waite Hill. He was but sixty-seven years old. Walter Murphy Halle was born on January 19, 1905, in Cleveland, Ohio, the son of Samuel Horatio Halle and Blanche Margaret Halle. After graduating from Princeton University, Walter joined the family business in

Outdoor dining at Halle's downtown (1959).

1927. Twelve years later, he became the general merchandise manager of the department store. He succeeded his father as president of Halle Bros. in 1946. Walter kept that post until his son assumed the role in 1966.

He married Helen Chisholm, descendant of one of Cleveland's most famous industrial families. They married in an Episcopal service at Trinity Cathedral. They had two daughters and a son named Chisholm. Walter served in the U.S. Army Air Force during World War II and was discharged with the rank of lieutenant colonel. Before he left for war, his children made him a bracelet that he wore for the rest of his life.

He was a tall, thin yet handsome fellow who was once named by *Esquire* magazine one of the ten best dressed men in America. His wife, Helen, was appointed by Jacqueline Kennedy to a special committee to improve the White House for special guests. He was a lifelong friend of *Cleveland Press* columnist Winsor French; when they were young, the two of them were sent to a boarding school in Wyoming. Walter served as a trustee or director for the Ohio Retail Merchants Association, Oberlin College, Cleveland Trust Bank, Cleveland Clinic and the Cleveland Orchestra. He passed away on January 10, 1972.[55]

Kay Halle

Katherine Halle, better known to her friends, family and fans as Kay, was born on October 13, 1903. She was one of five children of Samuel and Blanche Halle (Ann, Walter, Margaret, Jane and, of course, Kay). She was perhaps one of the most distinguished individuals to grace the twentieth century, wildly more popular than even her younger brother Walter. Over her many years of gracious living, she became a writer, lecturer and world traveler. Her parents enrolled her into Laurel School for her early education. In her teens, she attended the Mary C. Wheeler School in Rhode Island. Kay enrolled at Smith College for one year before returning to Cleveland and attending the Cleveland Institute of Music (CIM).

While at CIM, she studied with Beryl Rubinstein, famed pianist and director of the CIM. She also studied under Arthur Loesser, noted classical pianist and author. Kay moved to England in the early 1930s and was asked by the *Cleveland Press* to write a column. She did, and the column, titled "A Chair on the Boulevard," proved popular with Cleveland readers.

It was during this time in London that Kay met Randolph Churchill, son of England's famed Last Lion, Winston Churchill. Randolph became rather smitten with Kay, and both Kay and Randolph traveled across the Atlantic to visit each other. In fact, Winston Churchill decided to stop in Cleveland during one of his book tours in the States, wanting to make sure that Kay was up to snuff for his son. While Randolph pined for marriage, Kay's interests turned to broader matters. Yet for years she would show up at Chartwell, Winston's great country escape, to spend time with the Churchill family.

Upon her return to the United States, she wrote for the Paul Block newspapers. Block at one time published the *Pittsburgh Post-Gazette* and the *Toledo Blade*. She also wrote for the *Cleveland Press* again and the *Cleveland Plain Dealer*. Beginning in 1939, Kay started a fifteen-minute radio show called *Know Your City*, most notably broadcast on WGAR. She was also the intermission commentator for the Cleveland Orchestra.[56]

She was a well-known campaigner for Franklin D. Roosevelt but also attended the 1936 Republican National Convention with her dear friend Winsor French. French was a well-known newspaper columnist who wrote the society and out and about columns for the *Cleveland Press*. French actually included Kay in his will. While his million-dollar estate mostly went to friends and family, Winsor bequeathed Kay a modest $2,000.

The architectural design for a new Halle's escalator. *Courtesy of Western Reserve Historical Society.*

During World War II, Kay served as an executive in the Office of Strategic Services (OSS), which became the Central Intelligence Agency after the war. After the war, she decided to stay in D.C. but continued a radio show for WGAR called *This Week in Washington*. It was during this time that she became good friends with and confidante to many political and civic leaders, including Presidents Roosevelt, Truman, Eisenhower and Kennedy. Her home in Georgetown became known as Hotel Halle and was the headquarters for the young, the beautiful and the smart.

After World War II, she published two volumes of Winston Churchill's collected sayings and was the inspiration for persuading Congress to confer upon Churchill honorary U.S. citizenship. Her two books about Sir Winston are *Irrepressible Churchill: A Treasury of Winton Churchill's Wit* and *Churchill on America and Britain*. In 1968, the British government conferred on Kay the rank of officer in the Most Excellent Order of the British Empire.[57]

She wrote many articles and book reviews that were published in the *Plain Dealer*, *Reader's Digest*, *Look Magazine*, the *New York Times Magazine*, the *Washington Post* and the *Christian Science Monitor*.

She radiated kindness and brilliance. Kay was a tall, slender beauty who kept her looks well beyond middle age. She formed intimate yet enduring relationships with George Gershwin, Averell Harriman, Joseph Kennedy, Walter Lippman, Buckminster Fuller and, of course, Randolph Churchill. She kept a list of the sixty-four men who had proposed to her, none of whom could corral her independence. She was blessed to have grown up in an intellectually charged atmosphere that left her without prejudice or pretension and with an eclectic range of interests.[58] Kay would never marry. She passed away on August 7, 1997, at the age of ninety-three.

Chisholm Halle

Chisholm was born on April 8, 1933. He was a graduate of Harvard University. Chis married Ann Gelston King in the summer of 1955, and they had four children. His initial job at Halle's was to unwrap heavy boxes in the receiving department. He eventually worked his way up into merchandising and finally became president of the department store in 1966.

Problems began to arise at Halle's in the 1960s stemming from their over-expanded downtown store footprint and sales competition from other retail chains such as the Higbee Company and May Company. Chis did his best to improve the advertising strategy of the company, reform human resources and modernize the downtown store. He, without question, inherited challenging times at Halle's. The company was suffering from an overbuilt downtown flagship store and expanded too quickly into the suburban areas.[59] He understood the need to align the department store with a larger operation that had access to capital, offered a larger human capital pool and could improve operations at the Halle's chain.

Chis, with support from his father, Walter, was instrumental in selling the chain to Marshall Field in 1970. Whatever expectations he had of the marriage to Marshall Field surely led to disappointment. The executives at Marshall Field had promised Walter that Chis could stay on as president, but he was replaced by Paul Strohm, a Field's executive. Chis immediately resigned from Halle's and plotted his next move. In 1972, he and his wife, Ann, divorced.

He eventually opened Chisholm Halle's, an upscale clothing store on the east side, in 1975. His new store was the first tenant in the Eaton Square development built by Simon Properties. Chis wanted to create the premier couture store in the Midwest for both men's and women's fashion.

The Walker & Weeks architectural design for a new entrance on the corner of Euclid Avenue and Huron Road. *Courtesy of Western Reserve Historical Society.*

Chis married Cynthia, a former buyer at Saks Fifth Avenue, whom he met when she became a buyer at Chisholm Halle's retail store. A second Chisholm Halle store was opened in Fort Lauderdale, Florida, but was eventually sold to the management of the store. The original store in Cleveland closed in 1996.

Chis is remembered by friends and family as a man of great fun. Like his father, he was impeccable dressed. He set a huge fashion standard in Cleveland. He was an avid tennis player and loved to ski, especially at the family chalet in Aspen. He passed away on January 18, 1982, before the announced closing of the Halle store. He was but forty-eight years old, a life lost too early.

HIGBEE'S

The Best Location in Cleveland

The History

The genesis of one of Cleveland's most celebrated department stores didn't even begin in the city. No, it started in Burbank, Ohio—in good old Wayne County. It was in this bustling little village, a small center of trade that had a rail line pass through. It was there that John G. Hower and Edwin C. Higbee opened up a small dry goods store. Being the only such store in town, the two men made a good living. One day, Higbee was looking at the rail line in the small town when it struck him that the railroad was the one way out of town, but where did this line end? Yes, where did it go? Well, all good rail lines and canals and roads and trails seemed to lead to one place in particular.

Cleveland.

And so the two friends decided to jump on that train and make their fortunes in a real boomtown. On September 10, 1860, the small but enterprising Hower & Higbee dry goods store opened in the big city of Cleveland. The store was in a two-story building west of Public Square on Superior Street (now Avenue). The store employed five people, and business was beyond good—it was great.

The first day of business happened to coincide with the dedication of the Commodore Oliver Hazard Perry statue designed by William Walcutt. The statue was meant to commemorate Perry's glorious victory in the Battle of Lake Erie in 1813. The statue was placed on Public Square adjacent to the

Higbee Department Store on East Thirteenth Street and Euclid Avenue (1930).

new Hower & Higbee store. The crowds kept the two men and their five employees busy all day.

The two men were quite conservative with their business but felt blessed that good fortune had come their way. In 1863, they agreed to a modest expansion of their store. Yet by 1870, it was becoming quite clear that a new storefront was in order. The men moved their thriving store across the street to the south side of Superior (where the Renaissance Hotel is today). The new store at 238–40 Superior Street gave them ample space and the possibility of expansion. The two men improved the product offerings. The future continued to be quite promising.

Tragedy struck the partnership in 1897 when Hower died in a horse-and-buggy accident during the early summer. Higbee buried his friend and then became the sole proprietor of the store. The name Hower & Higbee remained until 1902, when Edwin incorporated the company as the Higbee Company and named himself president.

Higbee died of pneumonia shortly after in January 1906, but before his death, he asked his son William to assume a leadership role at the store.

William's first big decision came in 1909, when he decided to relocate the bustling store from its Public Square roost to a brand-new building at the northwest corner of Euclid Avenue and East Thirteenth Street. In January of that year, he signed a new twenty-year lease to move into the new structure. The plot of land the building was built on was quite historical, being the former homesteads of famed Clevelanders Amasa Stone and John Hay. The new building would quadruple the size of the Superior Street store.

William Higbee selected Abram Garfield, son of the late President James A. Garfield, as the architect for the project. While born in Washington, D.C., Abram moved to Cleveland after his father's death in 1881. He was the youngest child of President Garfield and Lucretia Garfield. He attended Williams College and received a bachelor of arts in 1893. He then attended the Massachusetts Institute of Technology and earned his degree in architecture in 1896.[60]

After receiving his degree, Garfield returned to Cleveland and joined forces with Frank Meade to form the architectural firm of Meade & Garfield. Garfield specialized in residential architecture, and a number of his designs are listed in the National Register of Historic Places. He designed his father's Presidential Library in Mentor, Ohio, as well as the Hay-McKinney and Bingham-Hanna Houses, which are now home of the Western Reserve Historical Society in University Circle. He was also responsible for the Leonard Hall dormitory at Kenyon College and the Mather House near Case Western Reserve University. Garfield was the architect for many homes in Shaker Heights, as well.

After his partnership with Meade dissolved in 1905, Garfield continued in a solo practice until 1926, when we created a new firm called Garfield, Harris, Robinson and Schafer. He worked there until his death in 1958. This firm continues to exist as Westlake Reed Leskosky Architects, whose offices are in the Hanna Building in Playhouse Square.[61]

In moving his store, Higbee was following the lead of Sterling & Welch and the Halle Bros. Company, which had both migrated to the Playhouse Square area. It was a location viewed as ideal at the time for serving the carriage trade. The new Sterling & Welch store had opened in May 1909, and Halle Bros.' new home greeted customers in 1910. The *Plain Dealer* lauded the move by Higbee's into this up-and-coming commercial sector by stating, "It is a sign that Cleveland is growing, growing, growing."

Higbee's also celebrated its golden anniversary in 1910. The growth of Cleveland's population, industry and wealth seemed as if it would never cease. Higbee's made the transition from a simple dry goods store to a trusted retailer. It was the perfect time to open such an opulent department store.

The façade of the new Higbee's palace was glazed white terra cotta and built at a cost of $350,000. It gave Higbee's 110,000 square feet of retail space on four sales floors. The first floor was an extraordinary open floor flush with women's fashion and a solid selection of menswear. The second and third floors were paneled in majestic white mahogany and offered up to the public as "French Rooms." The floors were packed with imported fashions from France and other exotic locations. The fourth floor was devoted to a stock room and administrative and billing offices. The whole building was fireproof.

William Higbee introduced eight new lines of merchandise after building the new store. These new products gave Higbee's ample retail ammunition against its favored competitor, Halle's, which had its own new store right across the street on the south side of Euclid Avenue.

In 1913, following the sale of Higbee stock to the H.B. Clafin Company of New York, William Higbee stepped aside as company president. In his place, the new board elected Asa Shiverick, a representative of the Clafin Company, as the new general manager of Higbee's. The Clafin Company was founded by Horace Bingham Clafin in 1890. His original dry goods store was based in Manhattan. Clafin operated as a wholesale business acting as an agent between select manufacturers and retailers of dry goods. However, the business model soon changed, and it was one of the original consolidators in the department store industry. Clafin acquired over thirty stores across the United States, including C.G. Gunther's Sons, the venerable Lord & Taylor, James McCreery & Company, O'Neill Adams Company, H. Batterman Company and, of course, Higbee's.

Clafin bought most of these retail chains by accumulating a lot of debt. In fact, when the company became insolvent and filed bankruptcy in June 1914, it listed debt totaling nearly $34 million. During Clafin's time in bankruptcy, the general manager of Higbee's, Asa Shiverick, went to the court to plead his case as a good owner of the business. He won, and the court awarded him controlling interest in the department store. The Higbee family, at this point, was still involved, as William Higbee continued on as a company director and vice president until his retirement in 1954.

After establishing financial control and stability of the company, Shiverick began to eye expansion. Higbee's had actually experimented with branch stores in the 1920s. One shop was located at Shaker Square (and then closed when the main Higbee's department store moved from

Higbee's fifty-foot-tall Christmas tree, outer portico of Terminal Tower (1968).

East Thirteenth and Euclid to Public Square) and the other in Ashtabula, Ohio. In 1922, Higbee's had to add another floor to its Euclid and East Thirteenth building, along with an extension to the rear of the store to accommodate new product lines.

The Shiverick years were generally good. He had a knack for merchandising and subtle promotion. But he lacked deep financial resources that could expand the Higbee's brand and financial position. Higbee's did OK financially but, more important, was widely considered one of Cleveland's most revered retail stores. Higbee's fortunes were about to be changed forever when a pair of notorious but secretive bachelor brothers came calling on Shiverick about buying Higbee's for a game-changing real estate development.

By the summer of 1929, the Van Sweringen brothers were getting frustrated by a lack of interest in their new department store building being constructed as part of their massive Terminal Tower project. So instead of trying to cater to the owners of such stores, they decided to buy one for themselves. In July 1929, the Vans tendered the Higbee board an offer of $7.5 million to purchase the company, an offer well in excess of the store's value. The deal was readily consummated, permitting construction to begin in 1930 on the new Higbee Public Square building.[62]

The initial site drawings for the Terminal Tower had an office building in place of a department store. These early drawings showed a fourteen-story Terminal Tower flanked on the west by the Hotel Cleveland and on the east by an office building. It soon turned into a fifty-two-story tower and a thirteen-story department store. When it was finally in the construction phase, the Vans were very particular about the materials to be used. Kentucky limestone covered the building, and granite was used on the ground floor. Prospect Avenue is actually a viaduct that was built over the Union Terminal rail tracks. The *Plain Dealer* called the building "a mountain of beauty built to serve every need for comfort and to meet every whim of taste."

In order to ensure a smooth transition from the "uptown" location at Playhouse Square to the new Public Square temple of retail, Higbee's announced a "removal sale" in July 1931. The new store would carry only new merchandise, so everything in the old store had to be sold. With the grand opening fast approaching, massive sales and clearances were a new way of life for Higbee's.

And then it happened. After twenty-one years on Upper Euclid, Higbee's returned to its roots along Public Square. It was September 8, 1931, and the new, dazzling thirteen-floor, one-million-square-foot retail store opened

Higbee's at Christmas (1955).

to a throng of shoppers. Inside the store, guests were overwhelmed with $5 million in new merchandise. It was an impressive opening for the store and the capstone for the Van Sweringen brothers as they finally completed their Terminal Tower vision. Over 359,000 people came out that day to see the new stores, but sales on the first day were modest. The Depression made everyone window shoppers.

The store had a weighty presence and fronted on Ontario, Prospect and the Public Square, with an unbroken line of sixty-five display windows. The May Company, Higbee's retail rival across the street, did not want to be outdone and had also increased its retail footprint as a means to compete. Landlocked by the Bailey Company to the south and the Park Building to its west, May Company could only expand up. A decision was made to build a two-story addition, making the store eight stories in all. May's new floors would provide the store with nearly 1.2 million square feet of retail muscle. It was still the largest retail store in Ohio.

But the new Higbee's building was a monumental form of architecture, making it difficult for others to compete. The Van Sweringen brothers had retained the Chicago-based firm of Graham, Anderson, Probst & White, who were also the main architects in the Terminal Tower project. From its basement shopping floor to the decks that received products daily to the stunning entrances to the womenswear on the second and third floors, reaching up to the art deco splendor of the Silver Grille on the tenth floor and finally to the WHK radio station on the twelfth floor, the building defied all expectations. Patrons could park their automobiles in the Terminal Garage entrance found on Huron Road and find nearly two thousand spaces. They could then walk through an underground passage through the Union Terminal into the Higbee store.

The building cemented Cleveland's legacy as an industrial titan on the American landscape. The total cost of the Terminal Tower project was a robust $179 million—over $2.5 billion in today's dollars.

New technologies were featured in the new home of Higbee's. A new telephone and mail shopping system was built that allowed any shopper to use their department store charge account to order items and have them sent to their homes—a real precursor to the Internet. Higbee's was also a part of the Charge-a-Plates program with the other five large retailers

Cleveland's "model community" on display at Higbee's (1946).

in Cleveland. The card was notched for the specific department store for which the credit was valid.

The building had twenty elevators that could take shoppers to every floor in the store (except the eleventh floor, which was reserved for storage). Escalators were in abundance, too, and gave the Higbee shopper an eye-opening experience with a vast array of merchandise available on every floor. Management got wise to shoppers' in-store traffic patterns, and many goods were neatly arranged near the escalators so that people might be enticed to get off on that floor and buy one more item.

But people weren't buying much in the haze of the Depression that started two years prior to the grand opening. In fact, in 1931, Higbee's lost over $500,000. And in 1932, the financial loss got worse, hitting nearly $3.5 million. Some of the floors were closed, and significant parts of the staff were let go. Higbee's willed its way to survival.

Behind the scenes, there were business decisions that were going to make life even more difficult for Higbee's. The Van Sweringens were mired in a financial abyss during the early years of the Depression. To help support their failing empire, the Vans transferred ownership of the department store to a new holding company called the Cleveland Terminals Building Company. It was an accounting trick that could not stave off the inevitable. In 1935, the Van Sweringens' problems were of national interest, with many thinking that if their massive empire failed it would make things much, much worse. There was no bottom. The brothers needed a bailout. A couple of close confidantes—George Tomlinson (a Cleveland friend) and George Ball—set up Mid-America Corporation and purchased the assets of the Vans' failed empire. Tomlinson and Ball then hired the only people on planet Earth who could help navigate the complicated connections and assets of the Vans' holdings. The Van Sweringen brothers were hired to manage what they once owned outright. Unfortunately, the brothers did not survive the renewal of their once glorious and formidable conglomerate. Mantis James Van Sweringen died in 1935, and his brother Oris Paxton died less than a year later in 1936.

During the summer of 1935, the holding company of Higbee's was part of a larger bankruptcy, and its future was cloudy at best. Asa Shiverick, president of Higbee's, applied to have the department store reorganized. The Mid-America Corporation, still the owner of the department store chain, had placed a defining restriction on the sale of the Higbee Company: the buyer had to be from Cleveland. Two brave Clevelanders stepped up to the challenge, both close confidants of the Van Sweringen brothers: Charles

Bradley and John P. Murphy. And yet it took a couple of years before the courts could clarify Higbee's financial situation.

Perhaps the one bright spot for most Clevelanders during the Depression came in the summers of 1936 and 1937, when the Great Lakes Exposition was held on the city's lakefront. If there was one definable, self-evident "Golden Moment" for Cleveland during the Depression, it was the Great Lakes Exposition. It started as a celebration of the Great Lakes' industrial might and pride but turned into a national affair that created enormous excitement and brought millions of people to Cleveland.[63] It was the brainchild of Cleveland's elite that was executed so brilliantly from concept to opening that it only took eighty days to ready the lakefront and create one of Cleveland's lasting memories.

The Great Lakes Exposition was grand in its scale. It was built on land extending along the lakefront from West Third Street to East Twentieth Street. All told, it was 135 acres that also included the Mall area, Public Hall and Municipal Stadium.[64] Work on the site started in April 1936, and eighty days later, the exposition was opened to the general public. A small city of 201 glowing, curving Art Deco–style buildings was beautifully perched along the coastline of Lake Erie. One writer called it "a city of ivory, a new Baghdad risen in the desert" (when Baghdad was still considered desirably

Construction of the new Higbee's store on Public Square (1931).

exotic).[65] Originally, it was scheduled to run for only one hundred days, but it proved so popular in 1936 that the city decided to open the exposition for a second run in 1937. Both Halle's and Higbee's had their own buildings at the Great Lakes Exposition. The Higbee Building was the tallest structure on the exposition grounds.

The Bradley-Murphy investment group consummated the Higbee acquisition on June 30, 1937. The purchase was eventually made from the George and Frances Ball Foundation, which had assumed all the assets of Mid-America. Any sales made on behalf of the foundation then helped finance its endowment. Tragically, two days after the transaction was completed, the president of Higbee's, Asa Shiverick, passed away. On the day of his funeral, Higbee's was closed so that all employees, managers and stakeholders could attend the ceremony. The other Cleveland department stores paid tribute to Shiverick by lowering their flags to half-mast. He was well respected and admired for keeping Higbee's alive and relevant during multiple bankruptcies.

A new era was afoot. Bradley became the new president of Higbee's and kept the post until he died in December 1945. John Murphy then assumed the role. The purchase price for the Higbee's acquisition was $600,000, of which $60,000 was in cash and the other $540,000 in a personal note by Murphy and Bradley. As part of the deal, the two gentlemen assumed over $1.5 million in Higbee debts.

With the passing of ownership of Higbee's to Bradley and Murphy in 1937, they assumed a twenty-year lease on the building, set to expire in 1950. The owner of the building was the Metropolitan Life Insurance Company. One of the key provisions of the lease was that the annual rents were based on the gross sales of the store. And with sales quickly improving under the new ownership group, the business was hit with steep rental increases, too. Bradley and Murphy were wise to this clause and in 1945 decided to exercise an option to acquire the building. The parties agreed to a purchase price of $8.7 million with $2 million down at close and the rest paid out in installments until 1949.

The connection between Higbee's and the Metropolitan Life Insurance Company started many years prior at Notre Dame. John P. Murphy was a student at the famed Catholic university and was friends with another student named Harry Hagerty. After graduation, Murphy found his way to Cleveland. Hagerty got a job at Met Life and worked his way to become a vice president at the company, in charge of the non–life insurance investments made on the company's behalf. This included the Higbee building, which

Met owned. In August 1949, Higbee's borrowed $3.5 million from the Met on an unsecured note payable over fifteen years.[66]

This wasn't the end of the financial relationship between Higbee's and Met Life. In 1961, Higbee's lacked the financial wherewithal for its aggressive suburban expansion and a necessary warehouse expansion, so it turned to its friend at Met. This time it secured a $9 million loan. And in 1967, an additional $19 million was granted to Higbee's from Metropolitan Life. It was a very financially successful relationship.

There were numerous clothing manufacturers based in Cleveland at this time. Cleveland was noted as a leading producer of men's and women's clothing. Higbee's had strong relationships with the city's best manufacturers, including Joseph & Feiss, Lampl's and Campus Knit Wear.

Higbee's, like Halle's, had a keen reputation as a purveyor of fine fashion. And to that end, its relationship with the American Merchandise Corporation (AMC) helped the store find and store merchandise on a global scale. AMC was headquartered in New York and was a buying collective made up of nineteen major department stores. The buyers of AMC bought quality lines of merchandise and delivered them to member stores across the nation. To access European products, known to be exotic and of top quality to American buyers, the AMC had established offices in London and Paris.

AMC was started by another retail legend, Fred Lazarus. Lazarus was born in Columbus, Ohio, in 1884. He began working in his family's small department store, F&R Lazarus, at age ten. He attended Ohio State University. He returned full time to the store upon his graduation and enjoyed one stunning success after another. In 1921, he founded the Retail Research Association (RRA), where all members had to maintain their financial books using accepted guidelines so that all members could share sales and profit information. Soon thereafter, Lazarus formed the AMC.

Years later, the RRA was merged into the AMC and became the research arm of AMC. In 1930, Lazarus joined forces with Filene's in Boston, Abraham & Straus in Brooklyn and finally Bloomingdale's in Manhattan to form Federated Department Stores. Lazarus took control of Federated in 1945 at the spry age of sixty-one. By the time he passed away in Cincinnati in 1973, Federated had over two hundred department stores.

A department store had to apply to become a member in AMC, and only one department store per city could hold membership. When accepted into membership, the store was issued a set number of shares in AMC. The expenses, however, were spread to the members/owners on the basis of sales volume. Taylor Son & Company of Cleveland was the original Cleveland member in the AMC but was required to sell back its shares when it became public that it was part of the May Company. Both Halle's and Higbee's applied. On January 31, 1946, Higbee's was notified that it had been selected to join the AMC, and it kept that membership until the department store chain closed.

AMC still exists and operates as a subsidiary of Target Corp. The company is one of three major apparel-sourcing and product-development firms serving U.S. retailers, the other two being Frederick Atkins and the Doneger Group. AMC spots trends; designs apparel, accessories and housewares; arranges for their production; and delivers the merchandise to its retail customers. The company operates more than fifty offices worldwide. Founded in 1916, AMC was acquired in 1998 by Dayton Hudson (now Target), whose chains included Target, Mervyn's California, Marshall Field's, Hudson's and Dayton's.

One of the benefits of being part of the AMC was that members could freely view great promotions and sales from other members in the co-op. The idea was simple: bring foreign goods and products—Irish linens, Belgian lace, Swiss watches, English silver—into the store and heavily promote the sale as an Import Fair. Ready to help was AMC's vast network of foreign offices to help select and buy quality merchandise from abroad. Higbee's launched its first Import Fair in 1956, and it immediately became an annual event with high expectations and robust sales.

After World War II, Higbee's was enjoying pent-up consumer demand for its product and services. The store literally could not contain the products it needed to serve this demand. So in 1948, Higbee's leased additional space in the main corridor of the Terminal Tower near Prospect Avenue. It was there that the store opened up the Higbee's Sporting Goods Store.

The old Higbee's store, too, was experiencing a new use with an old Cleveland retail name. After many years of inefficient use, the old Higbee's store on East Thirteenth Street became home to the consolidated Sterling Linder Davis Department Store. In 1933, the Cleveland Automobile Show was held in the former Higbee Building, displaying hundreds of cars to the public. During World War II, the U.S. Navy took over the former Higbee Building as its district headquarters. Sterling remained there from 1949 until 1968, when the store closed.

The 1950s were a magnificent time for Cleveland's Big Six department stores. Public Square held court with three of the city's best stores with Higbee's, Bailey's and May Company. A bit farther east on Euclid Avenue,

The exterior view of the Higbee's department store (1934).

one could find William Taylor Son & Company. And on Playhouse Square, you would find Sterling Linder Davis and the Halle Bros. Company. But there were many other retail stores to shop in as well. Numerous smaller niche retailers—some smart such as Bonwit Teller and others with more mass appeal such as Rosenblum's, Bond's or Richmond Brothers—also attracted shoppers. Cleveland was a fashion-savvy city. Both Higbee's and Halle's would change their fashion windows every Thursday. People crowded the store windows to see what the hot new fashion item was, and shoppers scoured the women's department for items to fill their closets. The May Company led them all in retail sales in Cleveland, while Halle Bros. was undisputed as the most upscale shopping experience around.

The battle between Higbee's and Halle's was ever present and perhaps the deepest rivalry of them all. Samuel Halle, his son Walter and renowned daughter Kay had created an aura that attracted many Clevelanders to their tony downtown store. But the rivalry between the two stores was rather refined. Higbee's management always took note of the newest products and services offered by Halle's. Halle's catered to the city's elite.

But Higbee's did have an ace in the hole. Higbee's literally sat atop Cleveland's transportation hub. The benefits of being part of the Terminal Tower were legion. Not to mention, the home of Cleveland's most popular radio station (WHK) was on the top floor of the Higbee Building. Higbee's, too, could count on its special relationship with Shaker Heights. The vaunted Shaker rapid transit line connected the village to downtown at the Terminal Tower. Higbee's was the most convenient downtown store for the upscale Shaker Heights shopper.

The true spirit of Higbee's was undoubtedly Murphy. Under his stern financial management, the store was fulfilling its destiny as a revenue machine. During his years as the captain of the store, sales increased from $28.7 million to $107.9 million. Higbee's was a profitable enterprise with annual profits climbing from under $1 million to nearly $3.0 million under Murphy's management. He was a civically minded soul with particular interests in music and the arts. His love of music was aligned with his financial allegiance to the Cleveland Orchestra and internally at Higbee's

Higbee's Bargain Basement (1931).

with the Higbee Chorale, a collection of store employees who would often perform at store events.

In the late 1950s, the store went through some necessary renovations. The eleventh and twelfth floors were re-created as a masterful music center in 1951. The store received new air conditioning, and a new candy store was added in this decade as well. Management did act wisely by adding new seating in the Silver Grille. Even the bargain basement received a face-lift in the 1950s. New escalators were added as well. Higbee's began a special Christmas tradition in 1952 when it placed a thirty-five-foot Santa Claus with flashing eyes above the Higbee marquee on Public Square. Mr. Jingeling, the famous Keeper of the Keys, became a Christmas tradition in 1956 at Halle's. He then became a Higbee's tradition after Halle's closed in 1982.

New traditions were launched in the store during the 1950s. The universally loved Import Fair was started in 1956. New products, foods and wines were introduced to the metropolitan shoppers of Cleveland annually at the fair.

Although the 1950s were considered by many to be the golden age of retail, there were problems lurking within the industry. The great expansion of department stores into the suburbs started in earnest in this decade. Higbee's competitors were expanding their footprints. Bailey's had opened two smaller branch stores in the suburbs, one near University Circle and the other in Lakewood. Halle's, too, opened two smaller stores in Cedar Center and at Shaker Square. Higbee's could not compete financially with its department store brethren unless it could break its own prejudice against geographic expansion.

The May Company and Higbee's were the last local holdouts on building branch stores in the suburbs. In 1957, that changed. May entered suburbia with its May's on the Heights store located at Cedar and Warrensville Center Roads in University Heights. Higbee's would most certainly jump into the suburban expansion game, and eventually the Higbee's marquee would be placed on fourteen stores in the Greater Cleveland area.

During 1960, Higbee executives discussed the possibility of turning its tenth-floor auditorium into a unique retail space during Christmas. And thus, Twigbee's was born. The idea behind Twigbee's was to offer a shopping area for small children so that they could buy gifts for their parents and families. Also during 1960, Higbee's celebrated its 100th anniversary. To commemorate this superb feat, the realm of womenswear on the famed second and third floors of Higbee's was remolded in a mid-century style.

Christmas still takes on a special significance for those who remember Higbee's. Every year, the movie *A Christmas Story* shows off the outside and inside of Higbee's. The extras in the scenes filmed in Higbee's were all employees of the department store. The filming of the Higbee's scenes started in January. An entire half of the main floor was full of movie sets. The film spent a couple weeks in the department store, and it was a big thrill for all the employees at the time.

The management of Higbee's kept the company on the sidelines for too many years regarding store expansion. Developers of suburban malls and shopping centers favored a Higbee's store as an anchor but had to wait. While expansion to the suburbs was discussed at the highest levels of the company in the late 1950s, it wasn't until the early 1960s that Higbee's began to devote time and capital to an expansion plan.

The first Higbee suburban store was at the Westgate Mall in Fairview Park. The contract for the site was signed in January 1961. The Higbee store at Severance was agreed upon as the first store, but development delays put the Westgate store as the first in the Higbee brand store portfolio. The Westgate Mall was owned by Anthony Visconsi, a Cleveland, Ohio–based real estate developer. On October 2, 1961, the store was opened to the public and proved very popular. Sales during the first twelve months exceeded projections by $4 million. Over the next few years, Higbee's took over multiple stores at Westgate. When the grocery store at Westgate closed, Higbee's took it over and created a Higbee's Budget Store. And four years later, Higbee's took over the Federated department store at Westgate and made it a Higbee's home furnishings store.

The next expansion store for Higbee's was at Severance Center. The shopping center was built on a large part of what was John Severance's estate. Severance was a Cleveland-born industrialist. He founded American Linseed Company, Colonial Salt Company and Linde Air Products. He is perhaps best known as being the namesake of Severance Hall, home of the world-famous Cleveland Orchestra. It was an expansive site, and in fact, the Higbee store sat exactly where the old Severances' mansion was once located. The site was originally developed at the behest of Walter Halle of Halle Bros. He wanted to place a Halle store on the site after he convinced Severance's nephew Severance Miliken to sell the site to a real estate developer. But the project was plagued by a host of department stores agreeing to move in and then backing out. At the end, both Halle's and Higbee's agreed to anchor the site, and the store was a very profitable unit for Higbee's until Richmond Mall was built many years later.

Higbee's Grand Tradition Party (1966).

Forest City Enterprises was planning the development of Parmatown and had polled residents of Parma and Parma Heights as to what department store they would like for the new shopping mall. Higbee's received the most votes. So in 1965, Higbee's started development on its new Parmatown store. After some stressful negotiations with the developer and May Company (which had wanted to restrict the size of Higbee's store), Higbee's agreed to limit the square footage it would build for a period of ten years. Higbee's hired Raymond Loewy & Associates as the architects. The store opened in the fall of 1968. Despite May's reticence at having Higbee's at Parmatown after the opening of Higbee, the May store experienced a significant sales increase after the opening.

Because of this, May's asked Higbee's to join them at the Great Lakes Mall in Mentor, Ohio. The mall was owned by Edward DeBartolo, who had worked with Higbee's before, and thus these partners made for an easy expansion of Higbee's at the mall. Other Higbee stores were built at Belden Village in Canton, Randall Park Mall, Euclid Square Mall and Beachwood Place. Higbee's also purchased the lease of the Halle store at Summit Mall in 1982. In 1986, Higbee's also opened a store at Rolling Acres Shopping Center in Akron after Montgomery Ward closed its store at the location.

Higbee's steady financial and operation condition was due to the strong leadership of John P. Murphy. Murphy led the department store as president and then chairman until 1968. His steady leadership through many challenging times embedded an inner strength built for longevity that few other retail chains possessed. Herb Strawbridge took over for Murphy. Strawbridge had started at Higbee's as Murphy's assistant in 1955. He took over as president in 1969 and later served as chairman of Higbee's until 1984.

The company went on an acquisition binge in the late 1960s. In the summer of 1968, Higbee's acquired Red Cross Shoe Store, which had a store at Severance Center. Later that fall, Higbee's acquired the Burrow Bros. bookstore chain—all fifteen stores. Another member store of the AMC, Dayton-Hudson, was a major investor in the B. Dalton Booksellers chain, and Higbee's thought they could duplicate that success locally. Burrow's was owned by Clevelander Howard Klein. After the acquisition, Higbee's closed a few stores that were losing money but also began opening new mall stores. The U.S. Department of Justice, inexplicably, filed an anti-trust case against Higbee's, thus forcing the divestiture of the Burrow Bros. chain to a syndicate of investors.

In the summer of 1969, Higbee's also purchased the stock of G.M. McKelvey department store chain, giving Higbee's access to the Youngstown market. Higbee's operated the downtown department store and a new junior's store that was spun out of McKelvey for a number of years.

At the end of 1969, Higbee's was one of only two department stores in Ohio that were still closed on Sundays. Given the competitive landscape of retail, it was decided in 1970 to open Higbee's for Sunday shoppers with the exception of the downtown store and Severance Center, which remained closed on the sabbath.

The Import Fair was so significant to Higbee's and grew with such vigor that by 1976, Higbee's was sending forty-eight buyers around the world multiple times during the year to find exclusive merchandise. Clevelanders loved the fair, and it became an iconic annual event for the store. The final Import Fair was held in 1980.

Like Halle's in Playhouse Square, Higbee's, too, became a real estate investor as a means to protect Cleveland from continual decline and, perhaps, create real estate development opportunities in the future. Higbee's interest in purchasing real estate started in 1972 after an article was published in the *Plain Dealer* detailing that the riverfront property where General Moses Cleaveland purportedly had landed was for sale.[67]

Higbee's at Severance Center (1963).

The only interested party was a junkyard owner. His plan was to junk automobiles on the land. Executives at Higbee's, and especially its CEO, Herb Strawbridge, were aghast that such sacred ground in the city would become a refuse heap.

So in December 1972, Higbee's acquired the Moses Cleaveland property. The plan was to build a public space and market very similar to Ghirardelli Square in San Francisco. While plans were being developed for this new "Square" in Cleveland, Higbee's started to expand its real estate holding at or near the east bank of the Flats. All real estate holdings by Higbee's were held in a subsidiary called the Higbee Development Corporation. Other investors in this holding company included Ohio Bell Telephone Co., East Ohio Gas Co. and the Northern Urban System Research Corp.

Higbee's acquired properties including the National Furniture Warehouse on West Ninth, the Western Reserve Building on West Ninth, the Bridge Central Hotel on West Tenth and the Seibert Building also on West Tenth. One of the fascinating side notes of Higbee's foray into real estate was the creation and launch of one of the first restaurants in the Flats. In 1975, Higbee's opened the Cleveland Crate & Truckin' Company at an old trucking terminal in the Flats. The restaurant's Beer Porch was legendary, and while the restaurant did not last, it sent the message that the Flats could be rejuvenated as a destination venue.

Higbee's also played a key role in saving the legendary Hotel Cleveland. After the hotel went into bankruptcy, the court appointed Art Model as the bankruptcy referee. Model asked a number of civic leaders to invest in the hotel property, including a $1 million commitment from Higbee's, and the hotel was redecorated and relaunched as Stouffer's Inn on the Square.

Sales at Higbee's continued to grow, reaching a staggering $246 million in 1982. But the growth came at a price, especially at the beloved downtown store. Higbee's chairman Herb Strawbridge noted that by 1982, the downtown store had 200,000 square feet of space that no longer had retail relevance. In fact, Higbee's rented out its seventh and eighth floors to Sohio, a Cleveland-based energy conglomerate, while the Sohio Tower, later the BP Tower, was being built on Public Square. Additional space was leased to the Women's Federal Savings & Loan on the first floor.

Strawbridge knew that corporate raiders were swimming in shallow waters nearby. At the end of 1984, two foreign investment groups had accumulated 48 percent of Higbee's stock. The two groups were Industrial Equities (New

Christmas event at the Higbee's Auditorium in downtown Cleveland (1973).

Zealand) and American Adventures (Netherland Antilles). Their presence at the board level was placing more and more pressure on the Higbee executives to cut costs, thereby impugning the customer experience—all for a few extra pennies added to the bottom line.

The real estate market in downtown was beginning to change as well. Forest City Enterprises concluded its purchase of the Terminal Tower and the Cleveland Union Terminal in 1983.

Robert Broadbent took over when Herb Strawbridge retired in 1984. Gene Nau then took over for Broadbent in 1988. This change of leadership brought about foreign control of the company. Nau and his team agreed to allow Industrial Equities to buy majority ownership of the company's stock. In 1987, Industrial Equities announced that it was going to sell Higbee's. It then sold Higbee's for $165 million to the joint partnership of Dillard's department stores and Youngstown-based developer Edward DeBartolo. The plan was to combine Higbee's with an intended acquisition of Horne's department store. The Joseph Horne Company, often referred to simply as Horne's, was an iconic regional department store chain based in Pittsburgh. The chain ceased operations in 1994 after being merged with the Lazarus division of Federated Department Stores, Inc.[68]

The stores continued to operate under the Higbee name until 1992, when DeBartolo sold his shares to his partners and the chain was rebranded as Dillard's. Costs were cut. The downtown store shrunk its retail floor plan, and the Silver Grille was closed to the public on December 22, 1989. More bad news was coming to the downtown retail environment. On October 16, 1992, May Company announced that it was closing its iconic downtown Cleveland store. Its last day was January 31, 1993. Higbee's stood alone. The Cleveland "Big Six" department stores were now more myth than reality.

On July 1992, Dillard's announced that it was buying out the DeBartolo family. Soon thereafter, Dillard's made public that Higbee's would carry the Dillard's brand. Higbee's was no more. Forest City Enterprises ended up buying the Higbee Building in 2000. And in late 2001, Dillard's announced that its Public Square store would close. The illustrious department store era in downtown Cleveland was over. Higbee's had left the ranks of the great iconic department stores, and yet the shadow of the store grows ever larger.[69]

Near the end, the once proud Higbee's store only had 105 employees servicing four floors of merchandise—not the ten floors that were, many moons ago, filled with the most exotic merchandise in the city. The store,

Another hectic day at Higbee's (1958).

renamed Dillard's, officially closed the huge building in January 2002. The Higbee Building was listed in the National Register of Historic Places and in the early aughts had the final retail anchor of the Tower City Mall with 120 stores—but the store's cache was long past. The Little Rock, Arkansas–based Dillard's could not muster the loyalty to the store (nor its customers) to provide the proper tribute to the old Higbee's name.

The Silver Grille underwent a stunning restoration in 2002 by the Ritz-Carlton Hotel. While the Silver Grille is no longer a functioning restaurant, it is open for many worthwhile private functions.

For a few years, the building was nearly empty. The main floor, second and third floors were restored in 2007 to house the new offices of the Greater Cleveland Partnership. In 2010, Dan Gilbert, owner of the Cleveland Cavaliers and Quicken Loans, announced that he had won a new gambling license and was targeting the old Higbee's Building as the new home of the Horseshoe Casino. On May 14, 2012, the Horseshoe Casino opened with two thousand VIP invitees enjoying the slots and card tables. A line wrapped around Euclid Avenue as an additional five thousand gambling enthusiasts were waiting to get their chance of winning big. The casino has changed its name to Jack Casino, but it is still operational and has given new life and vigor to the Higbee Building.

In 2018, Willoughby, Ohio–based real estate development company K&D announced plans to convert the fourth through fourteenth floors of the Terminal Tower (which formerly housed the Forest City Enterprises company) into market-rate apartments ranging from 600 square feet to 1,800 square feet. The fifteenth floor would consist of a gym, office space and a restaurant with a rooftop deck.

The Store

Higbee's large retail footprint offered a wide selection of goods and services that could rarely be found anywhere else. The store was, in fact, its own mall. Higbee's offered the world to Clevelanders. There was something for men, women and children to do and enjoy—be it the club-like Men's Shop, the Ladies' Lounge or Children's World, Higbee's had every shopper covered. Then the whole family would hit the refreshing Frosty Bar in the basement or head up to the Silver Grille for a more refined dinner. At its zenith, Higbee's store directory looked like this.

Basement

Clearance Clothing • Towels • Sheets • Gifts • Discount Shoes • Frosty Bar

Patrons could find the latest and greatest fashions at superb discounts in Higbee's clearance area nestled in the basement area of the store. Many shoppers walked right into the basement area of Higbee's from the Union

Terminal's east concourse, especially those who might be arriving via interurbans or Cleveland's rapid system. The clearance area could also be accessed from the main floor by elevators and escalators. And before anyone left the basement area, more often than not, they stopped at the Frosty Bar to enjoy Higbee's rich, delicious malts and crisp hot dogs.

Street Floor

Cosmetics • Fine Jewelry • Costume Jewelry • Fashion Jewelry • Diamonds • Watches • Gloves • Small Leather Goods • Handbags • Fine Handbags • Street-Floor Blouses • Tops • Scarves • Sunglasses • Neckwear • Hosiery • Slipper Bar • Street-Floor Shoes • Optical • Repair Desk • The Link • Men's Toiletries • Men's Sportswear • Men's Accessories • Men's Dress Furnishings • Men's Furnishings • Men's Tops • Stationery • Greeting Cards

There were four main entrances to Higbee's grand street floor: one facing Public Square, one at the Prospect Avenue end of the store and two along the Ontario frontage. Large columns dominated the floor as well as an overwhelming amount of merchandise. The floor was dominated by a

A Cleveland stag enjoying the sights and scents at the Higbee's perfume counter (year not listed).

commanding view of columns and a high ceiling. Glass-fronted display cases lined every aisle and were filled with stylish products. Another wonderful element of this visually delicious floor were the seventeen Italian fabricated crystal chandeliers that hung from the ceiling.

Prospect Level

Store for Men Traditional Shop • Designer Collections • New Breed • Men's Outerwear • Signature Shop • Men's Shoes • Men's Better Sportswear • Young Men's • Wines • Gourmet Shop

The mezzanine, or Prospect Level, was the smallest floor at Higbee's and offered a club-like atmosphere with men's clothing, suites, sports coats, shoes and hats. Other items sold on this floor included cameras, sporting goods and delicacies at the always popular gourmet shop.

Second Floor

Women's World • House and Town • Miss Clevelander Dresses • Miss Clevelander Sportswear • Stag Shop • Women's Shoes • Millinery • Wig Boutique • Junior Coordinates • Junior Dresses • Contemporary Juniors • Junior Lingerie • Junior Shoe Gallery • Bus Stop of London • Glemby Cosmetics • Hairwork • Le Bistro

Third Floor

Intimate Apparel: Daytime Lingerie • Nighttime Lingerie • Foundations • Leisurewear • Sleepwear • Loungewear • The Maternity Shop • Millinery • Misses Coats • Pacesetter Coats • Miss Clevelander Coats • All-Weather Coats • Better Shoes • Etienne Aigner Shop • Pappagallo Shop • Misses Dresses • Misses Sportswear • Casual Dresses • Pacesetter Dresses • Pacesetter Sportswear • Better Blouses • Sweater Shop • Active Sportswear • Status Sport • Sun Bar • Designer Shops: Little Couture • Mulberry Shop • One Step Ahead • Sportique • Country Club Shop • Designer Sportswear • Designer Shoes • Designer Dresses • Crystal Room • The Bride's Shop

The womenswear floors—the second and third floors at Higbee's—were collectively known as Women's World. A distinguished fashionista could not find a more discriminating collection of women's clothes outside of New York or Paris than at Higbee's. (With, of course, the exception being Halle's, just a short jaunt down Euclid Avenue.) The employees called it "Fashion Avenue" or the "Style Aisle." The center aisle on both floors was lined with women's apparel.

A Higbee's doorman mans his station in front of the company's store on the corner of Euclid Avenue and East Thirteenth near Playhouse Square (year not listed).

During the shopping spree, the female shopper could rest in the distinctive Art Deco furniture creatively scattered among the women's shopping floors. Young women about to enter college always took delight in shopping at the Higbee's College Shop. And for the discriminating young lady about to get married, there was the always divine Gown Shop, which featured the latest styles by some of the design field's foremost names.

The two floors were decorated with bespoke and rare woods, elements of ebony, walnut and imported oak (which was imported from old English estates to grace the magnificent Higbee interiors on these floors). Also on these floors were a shoe salon, a millinery department and a fur salon.

Fourth Floor

Health and Beauty Aids • Pet Shop • Customer Services • Fashion Fabrics • White/Elna Sewing Center • Children's World: Children's Shoes • Children's Sleepwear • Children's Accessories • Girls' Shop • Boys' Shop • Plum Shop • Infants' Shop • Infants' Furniture • World of Toys • Doll Shop

Children always wanted to make a trip to the fourth floor, which was a children's paradise: Higbee's Children's World. Clothing, toys, almost anything a young child or teen could want or need was found on this magical floor. The domestics department was also located on this floor and sold beddings, towels and blankets. During Christmas, the children's section of the floor was expanded to include the ever-popular Toyland.

Fifth Floor

Housewares • Cook's Kitchen • Bar Shop • Glassware • Crystal • China • Silver • Gifts • Figurine Gallery • Plant Shop • Shop of Old Things • Linens • Book Shop • Calculators • Business Machines • Cameras • Pro Shop • Sporting Goods • For Good Sports… • Perpetual Notion Shop • Home Improvement Center • Garden Shop • Luggage • Artist's Supplies

The fifth floor was devoted to housewares. The floor also offered women a refuge from the demands of shopping to rest and get refreshed. Higbee's famous Ladies' Lounge was an inviting venue with a collection of comfortable lounge chairs and tables. It was a club where women could socialize with their friends and acquaintances, write letters and simply relax. The restrooms were marble lined, and the sinks were made of pale green porcelain.

Another popular element of the fifth floor was the very popular and posh Higbee Book Shop. The shop offered a wide and wonderful selection of books from classics to reference books to more contemporary fiction. The shop held many book signings with well-known and not so well-known authors.

Sixth Floor

Draperies • Bedspreads •Rugs • Decorative Pillows • Floor Coverings • Lamps • Pictures • Picture Gallery • Decorative Accessories • Gifts Never Leave Home • Clocks • Bath Shop • Domestics • Art Needlework • Beauty Salon • Pianos and Organs

The key attraction on the sixth floor was the Beauty Salon, where guests could enjoy hairstyling, manicures, pedicures and steam baths. It was a marvel of Art Deco design with crystal glass ceilings and aged wood paneling. The Art Gallery was also on the sixth floor and always had a steady stream of art enthusiasts and collectors browsing the expansive art collection.

Seventh Floor

Connoisseur Gallery • Williamsburg Craft House • Furniture • Foxglow Gallery • Early American Furniture • Sleep Center • Pewter • Appliances • Entertainment Center • Music Center • Higbee Photo Studio

A manicure stand at the beauty salon in Higbee's downtown store at Public Square (1931).

When it was time to refurbish your home, you headed to Higbee's, took the escalators to the seventh floor and walked the numerous model suites that were built to display the wide selection of furniture. The model suites showcased furniture in room vignettes with the appropriate accessories. Higbee's had a large number of interior designers on staff that resided on the seventh floor ready to answer customers' decorating questions.

Eighth Floor

Form + Function • Café on Eight • Design Center

The eighth through tenth floors in the Higbee Building were smaller in size than the first seven floors and were, believe it or not, part of the Terminal Tower floor plan. The eighth floor and the eleventh floor were designed to be storage areas for merchandise. During the 1956 renovation of the store, escalators were installed, and the eighth floor was turned into a Garden Center. One could find everything from grass seed to lawnmowers on this floor. Will call could also be found on the eighth floor.

Ninth Floor

Customer Service Desk • Executive Offices

All of the executive suites and supporting staff were located on the ninth floor. These hallowed halls were where Charles Bradley, John P. Murphy and Herb Strawbridge presided over the operations of the store. The walls were richly paneled in walnut and were lined with etchings by Louis Rosenberg, who had been hired by the Van Sweringen brothers. Rosenberg was an American artist who produced hundreds of etchings of architectural buildings and structures in Europe and the United States from the 1920s to the 1940s. Rosenberg, at one point, had been hired by the Vans to document and draw progress on the Cleveland Union Terminal.

Tenth Floor

The Silver Grille • Winter Garden Restaurant • The Pronto Room • Twigbee Shop

The story of Higbee's wouldn't be complete without mentioning the famed Silver Grille. The restaurant was the ultimate destination for many Higbee customers, and it made the tenth floor of the store the place to be and to be seen. Many employees at Higbee's called the tenth floor Cleveland's Clubroom. Imagine visiting the Silver Grille, the Higbee Auditorium and the lesser-known Higbee Lounge after many glorious hours of shopping. It must have been spectacular.

The Silver Grille was originally a tearoom that featured "dainty food." Every large department store had a tearoom, and they were fashionably popular with the ever-growing middle-class women of the day. For example, Halle's had its Minotaur Room and May's offered up the Mayfair Room. The Grille was a popular destination for many of Cleveland's aristocrats, emerging middle class and celebrities who were touring through the Sixth City. Bob Hope and Ed Sullivan were spied at the Grille, cracking wise and enjoying great food. Every meal at the Silver Grille was an experience unto itself served on Higbee's custom china and coordinating placemats and napkins.

The original department store plan, as devised by the Van Sweringen brothers, had two separate restaurants on the floor. One was simply named the "tearoom," and the other was to be an octagonal men's smoke room. Given budget constraints, the smoke room was never completed. The room was designed in an art modern style. The Vans used their favorite designer on the Silver Grille: Philip Small of Small & Rowley. The furniture was selected by Louis Rorimer, who had designed furniture for the Statler Hotel, the Greenbrier, the Cleveland Playhouse and the Vans' home at Daisy

The children's bookstore at Higbee's downtown (1937).

Hill.[70] The Grille was redesigned in 1962 when a cage was built around the fountain, new flourishes added and additional seating was built out. The Grille could then seat 550 individuals for lunch or dinner.

The auditorium could seat up to 1,400 people, many of whom would gaze at the three-story-high translucent glazed ceiling. The venue offered both table and theater seating and hosted many special events over the years. It also doubled as the site for the annual Twigbee Shop, where children could visit with Santa, Bruce the Spruce or Mr. Jingeling.

Smaller meeting rooms could also be found on the tenth floor, including the Vista, Fern and Ontario Rooms. The tenth floor received air conditioning well before the other areas of the building.

Eleventh Floor

Storage • Employee Lounge

The eleventh floor was a storage and work area for store employees. A small retail area was eventually opened on the eleventh floor offering major appliances and the music shop.

Twelfth Floor

WHK • Higbee School of Music

When the building was originally opened in 1931, the twelfth floor belonged to Cleveland radio station WHK ("1420 on the radio dial"). In 1938, Higbee president Charles Bradley entered into an agreement with WHK that provided the store with a free hour of programming each week and at least four promotional announcements before 6:00 p.m. each day.[71] WHK was a pioneering radio station for the city and was an affiliate of the Columbia Broadcasting System (CBS). The station remained with CBS until the late 1940s, when it became a part of the Mutual Network.

In 1936, WHK was the first radio station to broadcast the entire Cleveland Indians season. Now the station focuses on nationally syndicated political talk radio, but then the station produced a large number of shows for all ages. WHK produced *Say It with Music*, the Louis Rich Orchestra and, of course, sports. When the WHK radio studios were being constructed, the Vans took into consideration television as a new technology.

In 1948, Higbee's, in partnership with RCA and NBC, built temporary television studios on the tenth floor of the store. Two large studios were constructed. One was two stories in height and could accommodate a symphony orchestra and five hundred people. WHK moved out in 1950, suggesting it needed larger facilities, and eventually decided on an old theater at East Fiftieth and Euclid Avenue.

With over twenty-two thousand square feet now at its disposal, the department store decided to build out the Higbee's Music Center. The old radio studios were transformed into fifty music rooms. Other areas were set up for Baldwin pianos and organs. A small concert hall was constructed that could seat 200 people. Thousands of Cleveland's children were taught music at Higbee's. Its School of Music could accommodate nearly 1,500 music students on a daily basis. In the Music Center, the record store had one whole area devoted to record-playing booths where customers could listen by earphones to their music selections. In fact, Higbee's Music Center became the model for a similar center built in the posh Harrod's department store in London. The Music Center opened in 1954.

Given the unusual structure of both the Higbee Building and Terminal Tower, Higbee's twelfth floor connects with Terminal Tower's thirteenth floor. The Vans had installed a doorway at this juncture, allowing them to sneak into Higbee's and enjoy lunch at the Silver Grille. But when going from

Charlton Heston signing books at the Higbee's bookstore (1973).

the Higbee Building into the Terminal Tower using this doorway, you would enter the Greenbrier Suite. The Greenbrier was as an eight-room suite that the Vans lived in while they stayed at the Terminal Tower and not their regular roost at Daisy Hill. It was a hidden enclave in a massive complex. The suite was also used by the Vans to entertain guests. It was constructed to look like an English country manor full of wood beams, peaked ceilings and oak paneling made from trees of Sherwood Forest.[72]

THE CHARACTERS

Edwin Converse Higbee

Born in Lodi, Ohio, to Jeremiah Higbee and Sarah Converse on September 7, 1837, Edwin was sent to public schools locally and then attended Glanville

College. At the age of twenty-three, Higbee moved to Cleveland and opened a dry goods and clothing company with his business partner John Hower. Upon Hower's death in 1897, Higbee became president and reorganized the business under the Higbee Company banner. He married Mary Elizabeth Haines, and they had five children together: Edith, William Tryon, Mary, Anna and Howard. He passed away on January 18, 1906, in Cleveland. William replaced him as president of the Higbee Company upon his death and in 1913 sold the company to a group of investors. He is buried in Lake View Cemetery in Cleveland.

Asa Shiverick

Asa was born in Omaha, Nebraska, in 1877. He was the son of Charles and Eleanor Shiverick. During his teens, he was sent to study at St. Paul's School in Concord, New Hampshire. It was there that he met and married Janette Bancroft. Originally hired by the Clafin Company out of New York, he became the general manager at Higbee's in 1913. He stayed in this position until his retirement in 1954. He was also a vice president of the J.N. Adam Company and a director of the Erie Railroad. Shiverick was a member of the Union Club as well as the Ellicott Club and Country Club, both located in Buffalo, New York. He had three children, Jane, Asa and Charles.

Charles L. Bradley

A Clevelander at heart and at birth, Bradley was born in the Sixth City on November 22, 1885. He was a student of the Cleveland public schools and University School. He was a graduate of Cornell in 1908. Bradley was the son of M.A. Bradley, who had in turn taken his father's shipping fortune and diversified it into a well-represented investment portfolio. After graduation from Cornell, Bradley took on work for the Van Sweringen brothers. During his tenure with the Vans, he took on more and more complex responsibilities. He was tasked with building the Terminal Tower complex and was chairman of the board of the Erie Railroad and an officer at the Nickel Plate Railroad. He was the president of both the Allegheny Corporation and Chesapeake Corporation. These were the two major holding companies of the Vans' massive empire.

Children riding the merry-go-round at Higbee's (1934).

After the Vans acquired the Higbee department chain and moved it into the Terminal Tower complex, Bradley and John P. Murphy were made directors of the company. Later, with the Vans' empire in ruins, Bradley and Murphy acquired Higbee's, and when Asa Shiverick died in 1937, Bradley became president. He held this position until he passed away in 1943. Bradley was also an owner in the Cleveland Indians. His brother Alva Bradley was the president of the baseball team and was instrumental in the construction of Cleveland Municipal Stadium and the move of the team from League Park to Municipal Stadium.

He passed away on December 19, 1943. He was fifty-eight years old. Bradley had two children, Mary and Alva. Alva joined the Higbee Company and was a long-tenured executive with the company.

George Merrifield

It was the keen fiscal acumen of George Merrifield that kept Higbee's from total financial ruin. Born in Boonesville, Kentucky, in 1883, Merrifield was born into poverty. By age eleven, he worked daily in the Stewart's Department Store in Louisville, and in no time, given his hardworking nature, he caught the attention of A.T. Stewart, founder of the chain.

Stewart is one of the lesser-known retail titans in the United States. He founded Stewart's Department Store in Baltimore and acquired Lord & Taylor in New York and Power's Dry Goods in Minneapolis. At one time, he even headed up Clafin's in New York (which owned Higbee's at one point in its history). Stewart asked the young Merrifield to join him in New York, which Merrifield did without ever having graduated from high school. It was in New York that Stewart discovered Merrifield's great financial talent.

Merrifield made his way to Higbee's during the depths of the Depression in 1932. He was named vice president and treasurer. He is widely considered the one man who saved Higbee's from bankruptcy by convincing John Murphy to become president of the department store upon Bradley's death.

Herb Strawbridge, Higbee's chairman, once said of Merrifield, "George was a demon for work and tiger for play." He loved Kentucky tobacco and bourbon. He loved to play cards, smoke cigars, enjoy the company of beautiful women, play the ponies and sing gospel hymns.

John P. Murphy

Murphy was born in Westboro, Massachusetts, in 1887. For college, he attended Holy Cross College on an athletic scholarship, and later, he received his law degree from the University of Notre Dame in 1912. Murphy was dear friends with Ray Miller, who would become one of the iconic Democratic bosses in Cleveland. (Miller's younger brother was the quarterback of the famed Four Horsemen of Notre Dame.)[73] Murphy was the athletic director at Notre Dame during his final year at the school.

He originally passed the bar and practiced law in Minnesota until 1915, when he moved to Montana and focused on railroad law. During World War I, he worked in the U.S. Army Air Corps and was commissioned as a second lieutenant. After the war, he was counsel for U.S. Spruce Products Corp. in Portland, Oregon. It was in Portland that Murphy meet Colonel John E. Morley, who was originally from Cleveland and on leave from the law firm Jones Day. Morley urged Murphy to come east to the Sixth City to continue his legal career. Another young officer in Morley's Portland employ was George Gund, who later would become CEO of the Cleveland Trust Company.

The Van Sweringens came to know Murphy and were quite impressed with his legal knowledge of the railroads, their largest business segment. From 1920 to 1937, Murphy served the Vans and worked extensively on their railroad and real estate interests. He served as a director for several of their companies. In 1924, Murphy married Gladys Tate. They had no children.

In 1937, Murphy became the sole executor of Oris P. Sweringen's estate, a challenging role given the expanse of the Vans empire and the financial crush they experienced during the Great Depression. Murphy partnered with Charles Bradley to acquire Higbee's. Bradley became the president while Murphy became secretary. Murphy also maintained an interest in his law firm of Morley, Stickle and Murphy.

He founded the John P. Murphy Foundation in 1960. Upon Murphy's death, the vast majority of his $13 million estate was added to the foundation's assets. The Murphy Foundation emphasizes education, especially in the secondary and higher education space, but also supports the arts, community and civic causes.[74]

John Murphy especially liked to help those who were willing to risk their own time, money and efforts in their endeavors. He found a true source of pleasure in seeing people have successful accomplishments of their personal goals. He loved amateur sports, opera, ballet, symphonic music, good literature and the Bible.[75] He passed away on July 15, 1969, at his home in Pepper Pike, Ohio. Gladys had passed away six months prior. They are buried together in St. Luke's Cemetery in Westboro, Massachusetts.

Herbert Strawbridge

Strawbridge was born on January 15, 1918, in Niagara Falls, New York, to Russell and Martha Strawbridge. It was a humble beginning to a grand life. At the age of twenty-one, Herbert (known to his friends as Herb) graduated with a bachelor of science from Purdue University in 1939. Upon graduation, he became a buyer at Montgomery Ward, the Chicago-based retail conglomerate founded by Aaron Montgomery Ward and Andrew Ward. Herb enjoyed great success at Montgomery Ward and spent fourteen years improving the buying process for the company. Herb married his beloved Marie on March 28, 1948. The couple had two children, Leigh and Holly.

He spent a couple of years as a retail consultant with Turton Associates, a Cleveland-based consulting firm, and that's how he connected with the Higbee Company. Higbee's retained Turton to complete some industry research. In early 1955, Strawbridge wrote a letter to John P. Murphy asking to interview for any position with Higbee's. Murphy granted the interview and came away impressed. In June 1955, Herb became an assistant to the president. It started a career at Higbee's that lasted until 1987. He became a vice president in 1959, vice chairman in 1962 and president in 1966. Later, in 1968, he became chairman of the company.

Herb was a member of the Country Club, Union Club, the Intown Club and the Clevelander. He was a founding or longtime member of core civic organizations such as Leadership Cleveland, the Greater Cleveland Growth Association, the Convention and Visitors Bureau of Greater Cleveland and University Circle, Inc. He was devoted to the causes and the financial foundation of the Kulas Foundation and the John P. Murphy Foundation.

He was a pioneer investor in the decrepit buildings overlooking the Cuyahoga River and in property in the Flats. Herb loved Cleveland, and Cleveland loved Herb. He passed away in October 2000.

Oris Paxton Van Sweringen and Mantis James Van Sweringen

If you were to politely ask a Clevelander today who the Van Sweringen brothers were, I suspect you might collect a few cross looks. On occasion, someone might offer that the Van Sweringens built the Terminal Tower complex or that they were the brilliant minds behind the creation of Shaker Heights. And these answers, of course, are true. Whatever you think of the Van Sweringens, you could never muster the belief of how powerful these men were. They were capitalists. Absolutely. They were industrialists. Indeed. They changed the look and, yes, the very prestige of Cleveland. No doubt. They were more than builders. They were the epitome of an early twentieth-century American capitalist trope: work hard and take big risks and you will be rewarded accordingly.

They were two of the most important people in the United States of their time period. Titans among mere mortals. Billionaires. Bachelors. The two brothers owned railroads, buildings, investments in industrial companies, hotels and, of course, a department store. Few in the world could muster the power and intelligence of the two brothers. And then… they disappeared, and so, too, did their gigantic business empire. They became ghosts. A whisper of what was. Shadows of the Sixth City. In fact, author and *Plain Dealer* columnist George Condon once wrote of the Van Sweringen brothers:

> *Of all the men and women to walk the Cleveland scene over the past 170 years, O.P. and M.J. Van Sweringen did more to alter the face of the city than any other private citizens, individually or in combination. They left a deep imprint that shows no sign of eroding. They were the builders of modern Cleveland.*[76]

Coming into the twenty-first century, they are nearly extinct from the Cleveland collective. That is a shame. With the exception of John D. Rockefeller, there is nary a better story (and cautionary tale) than that of Oris Paxton Van Sweringen and Mantis James Van Sweringen.

Within a twelve-year period (1923–35) the brothers Van Sweringen amassed a real estate development that included a completed community with its own government, a rapid transit system, a transcontinental railroad that was believed to be worth between $3 and $4 billion dollars and the construction of the largest building outside of New York. And then they were broke. Paupers of the Depression. Victims of their own success. True to their tragic script, one of the brothers died on his personal railcar with less than $3,000 to his name. The brothers dreamed big and yet were among the few in life to enjoy a reality much larger than what they could ever have imagined.

They were of Dutch ancestry. A family member of noble birth named Gerret Van Sweringen left Holland for the New World and settled in New Castle, Delaware. The brothers were born to James and Jennie Van Sweringen near the town of Wooster, Ohio. Oris was born on April 24, 1879, while Mantis was born on July 8, 1881. The brothers were inseparable their entire life—from childhood to death. The family moved to Cleveland in 1890 for a better life, and by 1897, both brothers were working for the Bradley Fertilizer Company.[77]

Both brothers were fascinated by real estate and by 1905 had invested in a Lakewood, Ohio development focused on Cook Avenue. The investment failed. The brothers, after a period of time operating a real estate business in their sisters' name, became real estate speculators in Cleveland Heights. It was speculation that brought forth new wealth for the brothers and a bold sense of accomplishment. With newfound coin in their pockets, the brothers turned their attention to Fairmount Boulevard, a stunning avenue but with little transit options, thus limiting the area's growth potential. The Van Sweringens used their private charm on the president of the Cleveland Railway Company to extend its rail tracks and service to their new subdivision on the boulevard. It imported a mission critical component to the Van Sweringens' future success: every one of their developments had public transit as a central part of the plan.

Soon thereafter, the brothers acquired the desolate and moldering ruins of the North Union Shaker Community, which had fallen on very desperate times. The ascetic Shakers established a fully self-sufficient farming settlement they called North Union on this land beginning in 1828. Doan Brook, which flowed through their property, was dammed for power, creating the lakes. Over the next twenty-five years, a stone gristmill, a large brick woolen mill, a sawmill, a blacksmith shop, a meeting house and communal living buildings all appeared as North Union grew and prospered. High-quality Shaker canned goods, butter, cheese, flour and yarn were also sold locally and were always in high demand.[78] The original landholdings held nearly 1,366 acres with sixty buildings. The North Union colony became a self-supported community that grew to three hundred members by 1850.

Fashion show at the Higbee's Auditorium (1958).

After the Civil War, the Shaker communities witnessed declining populations in all of their colonies. But Shaker celibacy and changing fashions in spiritual outlook ultimately doomed the enterprise, and so by 1889, there were only twenty-nine members left of the North Union Shaker Community. A local syndicate purchased the land in 1892 for $316,000. Shaker Heights entered the twentieth century looking increasingly overgrown and bedraggled; by 1905, its assessed value was almost 25 percent below the original purchase price.[79]

The brothers Van Sweringen bought the land for $1 million in 1905 and immediately began to develop the residential area that we now call Shaker Heights but then was known as Shaker Village. Their idea for the development was simple—build a terribly expensive, terribly exclusive and terribly desirable suburb. And in that, the brothers succeeded.

In order to transport the wealthy citizens of Shaker Heights to downtown safely, the Van Sweringens established the Cleveland Interurban Railroad. The railroad operated streetcar lines from Cleveland Heights to East Thirty-Fourth Street, but the track was incomplete at this point to its intended downtown destination. So the brothers had an ingenious thought—why not purchase a railroad to complete the Interurban?

It just so happens that a railroad was available for purchase. In 1913, Alfred H. Smith, a Cleveland native and then senior vice president of the New York Central System, made a deal to finance the Vans' rapid transit route as far west as East Thirty-Fourth Street, and work began in 1914. But at Thirty-Fourth Street, they were next to the tracks of the Nickel Plate railroad. The Nickel Plate consisted of a single 523-mile track between Buffalo and Chicago via Cleveland and Fort Wayne, Indiana. Built in 1881, it was outdated and had poor terminals and meager passenger travel.

In 1916, the Vans decided to purchase the railroad.[80] This fed the brothers' belief in the importance of building a public transit amenity into their developments. The Nickel Plate transaction also started the unique financing structures the Van Sweringens used to get their ever larger and larger business transactions completed. In short order, the brothers acquired other railroads, property in downtown Cleveland and holdings in Midland Steel, Goodyear Tire and Rubber and White Motor Company. By 1929, the Van Sweringens controlled over thirty thousand miles of railroad lines, including the Shaker Rapid Line, which was successfully finished in 1920.

For all their new ventures, the Vans, and their legal counsel, came up with a device that would let them keep their full extent of control with a minimum outlay for themselves: the holding company. The basic concept of a corporation that existed strictly to "hold" the controlling stock of other companies had been around for over forty-five years. Outside investors would supply most of the money needed to buy control of companies, they would receive either bonds or preferred stock that assured them an attractive fixed return on their investment, but they would have no voting rights and thus no control of anything.

It was a classic early form of what later financial writers would call a leveraged buyout. The downside, of course, was that the holding company had to pay the outside investors their assured return—which meant, in turn, that operating companies had to feed enough dividends into it to cover that return. Minimizing the brothers' personal financial stake while keeping full control of the various projects and operations was central to their method. The means were loans, the underwriting of projects by others and the latest and most promising method, the leveraged holding company.

One early investor was the young Charles W. "Billy" Stage, a former star athlete at Aldebert College and now a lawyer in Mayor Johnson's administration. Stage, in turn, introduced the brothers to another Mayor Johnson acolyte, the scholarly yet soft-spoken city solicitor Newton D. Baker. By this time, their inner council had coalesced into a tight handful, consisting primarily of Joseph Nutt, Charles Bradley, investment bankers

Warren Hayden and Otto Miller, banker John Sherwin and lawyer Frank Ginn. And they were heavily financed by Cleveland's Guardian Savings & Trust Company.

Meanwhile, in 1917–18, the Van Sweringen brothers built the Hotel Cleveland on their Public Square property. On the site of the Old Forest City House, the Vans constructed the new $8 million hotel. Once the Terminal Tower was built, many years later, they designed and built another $8 million wing to house a department store—and then bought the old Higbee Company to ensure a suitable tenant for the new store. This continued a trend by the brothers to acquire missing pieces of their business empire. Since they needed a department store and none would move to the new site, the Van Sweringens simply bought a department store chain. A new street on stilts was built south of the department store and terminal, and on it, the Vans constructed two new skyscrapers, the Medical Arts Building and the Republic Building.[81] One of the main reasons for the conservative style was the necessity of incorporating the Hotel Cleveland of 1918 into the group. When the department store was added in 1931, its symmetrical placement required that it also be designed to match the hotel.[82]

During the acquisition of the Nickel Plate railroad, the brothers stumbled into a grand debate over Cleveland's rail terminus. Most train service at the time in Cleveland would take place at the decrepit Union Station, which was at the lakefront bluff near West Ninth Street. The other smaller train stations servicing the city were clustered in the Industrial Valley along the Cuyahoga River. These stations included the Nickel Plate, the Baltimore and Ohio, the Erie Railroad and the Wheeling and Lake Erie. The goal was to build a larger Union Station at the north end of the Mall in downtown Cleveland. A bond issue was put on the ballot in 1915 and was approved by a 6–1 margin. But before any tangible building could be started, World War I broke out, and the plan was shelved.

The "war to end all wars" had unknowingly given the Van Sweringens time to contemplate and design a new Union Terminal—one that would support the Vans' new Terminal Tower project. The terminal and other new structures were planned to be constructed on the southwest corner of Public Square, which at the time was an area of high crime and squalor. In 1919, the public (enamored with the Van Sweringens' idea) voted for the redevelopment of the Union Terminal on the Public Square site, leaving the famous but competing Group Plan by Daniel Burnham forever incomplete. When the terminal project became a reality in the 1920s, the

Shopping at the dynamic and luxurious Higbee's (1963).

brothers decided to incorporate the Hotel Cleveland into the terminal group plan.[83]

It should be noted the vast scale of this terminal development. Downtown Cleveland before or since has not seen a construction site as large or as complex. The site covered thirty-five acres of squalor that fronted on Public Square and moved westward sloping down the hill toward the Cuyahoga River. The real estate held nearly twenty-two hundred separate buildings and housed a population of more than fifteen thousand persons. The Terminal Tower project was the second-largest excavation project after the Panama Canal.[84]

The master plan of the terminal development evolved into something bigger: Public Square was to become a major commercial and transportation hub. The initial design of a fourteen-story building gave way to development of a fifty-two-story structure. The deconstruction of the site began in 1920—with the new Hotel Cleveland beautifully positioned along Public Square—and included some of the city's most historic structures along with the shanty shacks and eyesores. The old American House on Superior Avenue fell, as did the Central Police Station on Champlain Street, the main building of the Ohio Bell Telephone Company and the famous Stein's Café. Complete streets, too, fell victim to the development and disappeared. Champlain Street. Hill Street. Columbus Street. Diebolt Alley and its famous restaurants—forever lost to history. Portions of three cemeteries also had to be destroyed, with the bodies removed and sent to various city cemeteries. Rail lines had to be rerouted to ensure that four different rail companies could use the Union Terminal, not to mention the Shaker Rapid extension.

The Union Station and Terminal Tower (including the Medical Arts Building and the Republic Building) took eleven years to complete. Actual construction began in 1923 and was finished in 1930. Estimated cost of the project exceeds $200 million. The Terminal Tower was expanded to fifty-two floors with a height of 708 feet and rests on 280-foot caissons. Designed by the firm of Graham, Anderson, Probst & White, the tower was modeled after the Beaux-Arts New York Municipal Building by McKim, Mead, and White.[85] For decades, the building was the tallest building in the United States outside of New York City.

To put it all in context, the 1930s witnessed several of the greatest undertakings in the city's history, which would influence the prestige, health and culture of Cleveland for generations. The Terminal buildings were completed and were immediately rated as the second-most important group of commercial buildings in the nation. A city within a city, the group embodied a tremendous railroad station, towering office buildings, Higbee's modern department store, Harvey's restaurants and shops, the famous Hotel Cleveland, a monumental post office and offices of major banks.[86]

Many interested parties thought of the Vans at best as well-dressed gamblers and at worst as speculators. Yet they were nothing if not long-term builders. In their first real estate ventures, they held and developed properties over what were considered absurdly long periods. It took over twenty years just to physically complete the Public Square–Union Terminal project, and it was a year more before it became commercially productive—and what was completed was only part of a larger plan. Their suburban developments in Shaker Heights and beyond were planned to mature over a period of about twenty-five years.[87] In almost all of their business deals and transactions, the Van Sweringens bought undervalued properties, put all the money into them that could be afforded and built them up slowly; many were made into models of operational efficiency and service quality.[88] Yet the brothers did stretch the law and corporate structures about as far as they could go. There were justified accusations of lapses in corporate ethics and shadowy legal subterfuges that were questionable even by the more freewheeling business standards of the 1920s.[89]

At their financial zenith, the brothers' holdings included 231 companies with assets valued between $3 and $4 billion. Included in these properties were twenty-four railroads, large real estate holdings, coal operations, hotels and other affiliated companies. With the Van Sweringens' wealth beginning to evaporate during the Depression, *Fortune* magazine printed a story in 1934 analyzing the brothers and noted:

> *The Van Sweringen brothers are conveniently regarded by the business world as one man. And with some reason. For no two men of their prominence have ever so successfully merged their identities. If they had been joined like Siamese twins, they could scarcely be any closer.*

Real estate being their first love, it is not surprising that the brothers enjoyed their own personal holdings as well. As part of their Shaker Heights development, the two brothers purchased a rather spectacular English Tudor at 17400 South Park Boulevard. In addition, when enjoying the spoils of downtown, the brothers called the Greenbrier Suite home. Located on the thirty-sixth floor of the Terminal Tower, the Greenbrier Suite was an amazing personal residence in a tower built for big business. The Van Sweringens also owned three luxurious private railway cars fitted with the best modern amenities at the time. But perhaps their favorite place on earth was Daisy Hill, their sprawling 660-acre expanse in Hunting Valley, just fifteen miles east of Cleveland.

Over the years, the Van Sweringen brothers had purchased four contiguous farms to create Daisy Hill. The farms lost all their commercial productivity, yet the brothers found a peaceful oasis away from their growing and complex business empire. The estate included a stable, four living suites, a carpenter shop, a machine shop, twenty-two garages, a nursery, a greenhouse and a man-made lake. It took seven years to complete and cost over $3 million. When the furnishings were sold at a four-day auction sale in 1938 by the Parke Bernet Galleries, a 220-page catalogue was needed to list and describe the 1,250 items offered.[90]

The boys were not involved in any social set and frowned upon being in the media. While they had national interests, they preferred to stay close to the Cleveland area. The Van Sweringens were members of Union Club, Shaker Heights Country Club and Pepper Pike Country Club but rarely participated in the clubs' social offerings. They were best friends and inseparable.

On June 28, 1929, a formal dedication was held for the opening of the grand Terminal Tower complex, including the Hotel Cleveland, which had been built many years earlier. It was a grand celebration that included governors, senators, cabinet members and entertainers—a veritable who's who in the world, with the exception of the Van Sweringen brothers, who decided to dine alone at Daisy Hill. It was their pinnacle moment. (Prior to the completion of the Terminal Tower, the tallest building in Cleveland was the "Temple to Telephony," otherwise known as the Ohio Bell Telephone Building. This stunning "Temple" housed Ohio Bell's executive and business offices, as well as telephone equipment. The modernistic, limestone-clad tower rose twenty-two stories, dominating the Huron Road–Prospect Road area.)

Not four months later, the Great Depression was beginning to take form over the United States. And the Van Sweringens' vast fortunes were not immune to its effects. By 1930, they controlled thirty thousand miles of railroads reaching from the Atlantic to the Rockies and from Ontario to the Gulf of Mexico, plus trucking companies, shipping companies and warehouses—and they had planned and built two nationally admired models of innovative urban and suburban development.[91]

The Center Stage Singers performing at the Higbee's Auditorium (1975).

The cracks started to show almost immediately in the Van Sweringens' financial empire. The main source of revenue for the Van Sweringens' conglomerate leviathan was not the real estate holdings but rather the railroad businesses. And the railroads were hit hard by the Depression. In less than two years, the Van Sweringens' railroad revenue dropped by nearly 50 percent. In the early months of 1930, the brothers turned to J.P. Morgan for financial support, and the investment bank loaned the Van Sweringens $40 million.

By 1935, it was becoming evident that the loan was not going to be repaid, and an auction was called to liquidate the Van Sweringen holdings. At the loan auction, which Oris did attend, nearly $3 billion worth of assets and companies, then employing nearly 100,000 during the Depression, were acquired for $3,121,000. All of this was acquired by a company named Mid-America Corporation. Mid-America's owners were friends of the Vans—notably George Ball, George Tomlison and the Midland Bank of Cleveland. The new owners of the failed Van Sweringen business behemoth hired the two best individuals for the job: Oris and Mantis Van Sweringen. The brothers were told to take $75,000 a year in salaries, and that would be matched by other gifts of $75,000.

Mantis began to have serious health issues in 1935 and died the morning of December 13. His brother Oris, heartbroken and lost, was quoted as saying, "I don't know what to do, or how to do it, or where to go from here."

Oris lived less than a year after Mantis's passing. He died on his personal train near Hoboken, New Jersey. It seems fitting that the brothers share a cemetery plot at Lakeview Cemetery under a tombstone that reads, "Brothers." However, the Vans' empire was beginning to earn profits again, and it seemed, at least in 1936, that it might defy the odds and be reborn as the goliath it once was.

The two brothers were indeed the architects of the grand Cleveland that has slowly eroded over the years. But their imprint remains. Anyone walking around downtown can immediately fall under the spell of the hypnotic beauty that is the Terminal Tower, the Higbee Building and the Hotel Cleveland. But the brothers also created Shaker Heights (often considered the best planned development ever in the United States) and parts of Cleveland Heights and even developed a small strip of properties in Lakewood. In addition, for a brief shining moment, the brothers were owners of the largest railroad company in the country. It is difficult to aptly describe the two men, who were so connected by the bounds of brotherhood, but perhaps the best way to detail who they might have been would come from an old Winston Churchill quote: "It is a riddle, wrapped in a mystery, inside an enigma." And, of course, that would make the brothers smile.

MAY COMPANY

Ohio's Largest Store

The History

Commodore Beaumont steps out of the warm confines of the E.R. Hull & Dutton Company on Ontario Street. For a few moments, he looks around at all the people on the street. He hears music from a nearby salon. Streetcars take people back to their homes for the evening. He must find a nearby Western Union storefront and message his brother-in-law David May. May is early in his arc of building one of America's most well-known department stores. Cleveland is a perfect city to buy his way into the game. Beaumont believes he has negotiated a deal to acquire the Hull & Dutton dry goods store. May must be notified before other buyers slip into the equation. Beaumont is amazed by the energy of Cleveland. It is a city willing to offer large fortunes to brave souls. Beaumont catches his breath, turns north on Ontario and heads toward Superior Street. He disappears into the night.

The May Company, destined to become "Ohio's Largest Store," was founded in 1899 when David May and his associates purchased the well-known store of the E.R. Hull & Dutton Company in Cleveland. May acquired Hull & Dutton for $300,000. The May Company of Cleveland was the third store in the nationwide organization known as the May Department Stores Company. The company, founded near Denver in 1877, opened the first May store in the mining town of Leadville. May was twenty-nine years old at the time.

May was born in Germany and immigrated while a teenager to Indiana. While in Indiana, he was a salesman in a small men's clothing store. May was blessed with an iron will and marketing flair—and soon earned a quarter-interest in the retail storefront. The brutal Indiana winters tested his frail constitution, and one of his doctors mentioned the fresh air and moderate climate of Colorado.

Out west, he tried his hand at prospecting but failed miserably. May returned to the comforts of retailing. With two other partners, he launched a new retail enterprise—May, Holcomb & Dean—that supplied miners with red woolen underwear and copper-riveted overalls and jeans. A real estate disagreement with his other partners led to the dissolution of the partnership. His second retail store, the Great Western Auction House & Clothing Store, was yet another retail success. Another branch store was added in Aspen.

The May Company grew to include other large stores and a number of branches, each operating independently under its own management. In fact, the May Company originated the concept of a retail holding company that bought, sold and merged regional department stores that typically operated under their original brands, such as Foley's and L.S. Ayres. For most of the company's history, the operations of various divisions were kept separate.

By 1885, May's corporate strategy was beginning to take shape. Print advertising that trumpeted genuine bargain prices enticed an ever-expanding middle-class clientele, while frequent sales kept the merchandise moving.[92] Some popular annual sales events held at the Cleveland store included massive furniture sales, the Great May Sale, Summer White sales and the occasional fashion clearance. There were even particular sales for silks and furs. Heavy investments were made in May's extensive purchasing network. Each May Company store had its own buyers, and these buyers served the specific needs of the local community with focused product selections.

May also looked to acquire other retail stores in cities or markets that were flush with immigrants and industry. He acquired the Famous Department Store in St. Louis in 1892. In 1905, the May Company moved its headquarters to St. Louis, where it remained until the 1990s.

Back in Cleveland, a flourishing clothing and furnishing store known as E.R. Hull & Company, located on the west side of Ontario Street at Champlain Street (later to be part of the Higbee building in the Terminal Tower development by the Van Sweringen brothers), was being operated by E.R. Hull and his associates J.C. McWater and Samuel E. Gravves. The firm was reorganized in 1890 when William F. Dutton of Baltimore joined Hull in establishing the E.R. Hull & Dutton Company. Hull & Dutton was

Sunny day on Public Square, looking south toward Euclid Avenue and the May Company (1915).

famous for its advertising stunts, offering prizes ranging from baseballs and bags to ponies and carts as premiums.

After the acquisition, the store moved across the street into a new six-story building. Hitching posts were at a premium in the neighborhood; there were too many shoppers and too few spaces for parking horses. A one-story building on Euclid at the southeast corner of a narrow street (East First Street) served as an annex and was the modest beginning of the May Company's future Public Square frontage. The Ontario store had as neighbors to the north the Cleveland Dry Goods Company and the W.P. Southworth Company, while east of the annex on the square were William Taylor Son & Company, Crow & Whitmarsh and Sterling & Welch.

However, May and his brother-in-law Colonel Louis Beaumont had been seeking an opportunity in Cleveland as early as 1898. Soon after buying the storefront, May and Beaumont hired E.M. McGillin to become general manager. In the summer of 1899, May Company's board of directors voted to demolish the store's annex and replace it with a modern eight-story facility. May hired the Cleveland-based architectural firm of Knox & Elliot to design and build the new facility. The building used a semi-fireproof structure and a terra-cotta veneer with decorative large plate-glass windows.[93]

The site of the May Company on Euclid Avenue (facing Public Square) was once the imposing residence of Richard Winslow, who owned a wholesale grocery store on Superior Street. Winslow's residence was built by Levi Johnson. Johnson was well known in Cleveland for building ships and residences for the wealthy and elite. He built Cuyahoga County's first courthouse and jail on the northwest corner of Public Square in 1812, an inn named the Johnson House in 1852 and Cleveland's first lighthouse in 1830.

And in 1868, on the very same May Company site facing Euclid Avenue, William C. Rudd and George H. Chandler formed Chandler & Rudd, operating a small store facing the south side of the square. The store specialized in fruits and vegetables. By 1870, the Cushing Block had been erected by Dr. Henry K. Cushing. It was a four-story building on the south side of Public Square (situated on the eastern portion of the May Company site). Prominent tenants were the Standard Oil Company and Cleveland's water works department. In 1870, Taylor, Kilpatrick & Company (later Taylor Son & Company) opened a dry goods store on the first floor of the Cushing Block.

On the site of the future May Company store, located just south of Euclid Avenue on the east side of Ontario, the S.S. Kresge store in Cleveland opened its doors to the public in May 1905. Kresge eventually moved to the corner of Euclid Avenue and East Fourth Street where the Corner Alley restaurant and bowling alley are today.

One of May's brothers-in-law, Louis B. Beaumont, assumed management of the store. As the store expanded, Beaumont first leased and then bought a shoe operation that was operated by Nathan Dauby. Beaumont made Dauby general manager of the facility, while he became the president of the Cleveland store. Dauby was fanatical about pricing products appropriately; he knew when to put an item on sale and when not to. He was the first to use escalators for a retail store in Cleveland, and he established the Eagle Stamp loyalty program. All told, he spent nearly sixty years at the May Company store in Cleveland.

In 1901, May acquired property on Euclid Avenue on the south side of Public Square, increasing its floor space from 73,000 to 131,000 square feet. Rapid and consistent growth resulted under the leadership of Nathan Dauby. The store expanded ten times after its original opening until it occupied more than one million square feet, and plans for further remodeling were underway in the later 1940s. Also, in 1901 the May Company introduced "special delivery service by the 'White Flyer' truck."

May opened a new storefront just for shoppers when it began the early morning sales specials. These sales were heavily hyped in all the daily newspapers in Cleveland and the surrounding areas. Patrons flocked to the store when the sales were available. The May Company, in 1907, refurbished a nearby Euclid Avenue building that once housed the William Taylor Son & Company store before Taylor moved farther east on Euclid.

The store found new ways to support its employees as it established an employee benefit society known as the Mutual Benefit Association. The association provided employees with up to $6 a week for an illness and a $100 death benefit.

To fuel its growth, the executives at the May Company had decided to go public. With board approval, the company hired Goldman Sachs and Lehman Brothers to help it sell its equity to institutional investors. May was listed on the New York Stock Exchange in 1911. Some of the stock proceeds went to the acquisition of the William Barr Dry Goods Company.

In 1912, the May Company acquired M. O'Neil department store in Akron. The O'Neil department store was founded in 1877 by Michael O'Neil and Isaac Dyas. This acquisition helped May improve its retail position in northeast Ohio. Later, the company announced in 1913 that it was going to build a new May Company store on Euclid Avenue in Cleveland. This $3 million expansion included a new building that would extend from Public Square to Prospect Avenue.

The new May Company store was finished and opened to the public in 1915. This grand shopping palace had over 800,000 square feet of retail space. At the time, it was believed by the local daily press that it was

Original May Company Building on Euclid Avenue next to Taylor & Sons (year not listed).

the third-largest store in the country. The store was designed by Daniel Burnham, the world-famous architect who designed Cleveland's group plan and public mall. The building was designed in the City Beautiful movement, or Commercial style, made famous by Burnham. The City Beautiful movement was a reform philosophy of North American architecture and urban planning that flourished during the 1890s and 1900s with the intent of introducing beautification and monumental grandeur in cities. Cleveland was the center of the City Beautiful movement, as were Detroit, Chicago and Washington, D.C. The movement promoted beauty in architecture not just as an ornamental appendage but rather as a means to create a moral code and ensure civic virtue.

The May Company building, now located at 158 Euclid Avenue, was an eight-story metal-framed, terra cotta–faced mercantile structure. At the roofline were a series of akroteria (an architectural ornament placed on a flat pedestal called the acroter and mounted at the apex or corner of the pediment of a building), a scrolled pediment and a clock in the prevailing Renaissance Revival style, all from the original building. It is a significant example of the work by D.H. Burnham and Company, one of four buildings by Burnham in the city of Cleveland and one of the most characteristic examples of the Commercial style fostered by the Chicago School of

Architecture.[94] The building offered all the elegances that became tried and true for Burnham. The façade of the building was a gleaming white terra cotta finish. Burnham used a steel and concrete frame that allowed for the generous use of "Chicago-style" windows facing Cleveland's pride and joy: Public Square.[95]

The store offered for sale every imaginable item—furniture, clothing, housewares, hats, furs, jewelry and shoes. The May Company store also offered a soda fountain, an auditorium, a hair salon, a children's playground (Playville in the Playground) and restaurants, all accessible by twenty-three passenger elevators. The playground area had a large sandbox, a clown who would walk a dog along a tightrope for the children's amusement and a large playground-size silver metal slide.[96] The playground also featured toy train rides and a merry-go-round. The playground could accommodate 250 kids. It was a spectacular service and feature for shoppers who could leave their kids at the attended playground and go shopping.

Men took to the store as well, as the new May Company store provided an indoor driving range and professional putting greens. Free eye examinations and amateur tennis matches were often offered to the public. The store even had a built-in U.S. post office branch so that sending gifts became quite easy. The vast store had to be serviced by nearly 2,300 employees. One of

The May Company Accordion Concert Band, Mr. Joseph Monia, conductor (1940).

the plum jobs at May Company was the elevator operator position. All the elevator girls wore crisp, elegant uniforms and white gloves.[97] They were taught to stand with the perfect posture, to look straight ahead and call out each floor.

In 1917, May elevated his son Morton to the presidency of the overall holding company. May became chairman of the board and continued to acquire other regional retail chains. The Roaring Twenties helped grow the retail market not just in Cleveland but nationally as well. May Company felt it had to offer new services to its ever-expanding middle-class target market. During the 1920s, the store began to offer a same-day dry cleaning service and a new bakery.

The automobile, too, was having a dramatic effect on where people shopped. To enhance its parking situation (since the store was essentially landlocked—both May Company and Bailey's Department Store took the entire Euclid Avenue, Ontario Avenue and Prospect Avenue block), May decided to build a new parking garage. The structure was completed in 1924 on the corner of Lakeside Avenue and Ontario Street. The architects on the project were Lehman & Schmidt from Boston. May Company also provided a free shuttle service to and from the garage. The garage even had a special room for all the chauffeurs.[98]

By 1926, May Company nationally had earned over $100 million in revenue. May had built a successful, vibrant national retail powerhouse. He passed away in 1927 at the age of seventy-nine.[99] The nation mourned.

In 1929, it was decided to expand the restaurant within the downtown Cleveland store. The new Spanish Room Restaurant and Tea Room opened to rave reviews. The store was an immediate success and by 1931 had to expand to meet customer demands. In 1931, the Public Square store added two additional floors, increasing the available retail space to over one million square feet. Patrons could enjoy the famous May Company Frosty Malted chocolate shakes in the basement area or treat themselves to a classic lunch at the Three Crowns Restaurant on the fifth floor. A year later, the Cleveland store installed a new $1 million air conditioning system.

During the Depression, the May Company survived by a strict compliance to financial planning and a strong investment in inventory. Despite the economic conditions, management at May felt it was important that any customer who walked into the store had a vast array of products available to them. The strategy worked. The May Company's extensive buying power and vast distribution network enabled the store executives to offer items not readily found elsewhere.[100]

The Depression took its toll on the May Company's finances in Cleveland to be sure. But the store held up better than most. Its unrivaled buying capacity and heavy investment in services really supported the store's customer base until better financial times would materialize. Customer service options at the downtown Cleveland store included a large waiting room, a lending library, a luxury travel agency, a very popular beauty salon, a religious or ecclesiastic department, the post office, a large check room, dry cleaning and free gift wrapping service.

Christmas was a special time for the retailers of Cleveland. During certain holiday seasons, a huge cross, 160 feet high and 80 feet wide, formed by red lights in windows of the Terminal Tower attracted citywide attention. The May Company, in 1934, provided a massive Christmas tree for Cleveland to be placed on Public Square.[101] The tree was enthusiastically received, and the store continued the custom every year, its trees standing majestically on Public Square. It turned the square into a winter wonderland. The bells of the Old Stone Church and the May Company Christmas tree brought holiday cheer to thousands.[102]

As the Depression began to dissolve, acquisitions started anew. In 1939, the May Company acquired majority control of another Cleveland department store, William Taylor Son & Co., which maintained its name until 1961. This occurred when Taylor Son's president and largest shareholder of the store, Sophia Taylor, passed in 1936. Her estate mandated that the store begin selling her stock. May Company entered into discussions with Taylor's estate and acquired 49 percent of the Taylor Son & Company common stock and 54 percent of the preferred shares available. May also acquired the option of purchasing all of the remaining shares at a future date.

In 1946, May Company acquired the Kauffman retail chain based out of Pittsburgh. Strouss-Hirshberg Company followed in 1948. The Strouss-Hirshberg acquisition cost the May Company $5,700,000 and solidified May's presence in Cleveland, Akron, Youngstown and Pittsburgh—the industrial heart of the country.

Expansion to the suburbs began in the 1950s, starting with the Sheffield Shopping Center in Lorain. The store was originally opened as an O'Neil's department store. O'Neil's at the time was a May Company subsidiary. This store became a May Company store in 1967. Nevertheless, customers flocked to the new store, which was designed by the Cleveland architectural firm of Weinberg & Teare. The store was 157,000 square feet designed in a Midcentury Modern form. This O'Neil's store was the anchor for the new $10 million Sheffield Centre shopping mall.

May Company–sponsored World Series scoreboard for the 1938 World Series.

The company offered a unique and groundbreaking food service for any customer who would buy a Westinghouse refrigerator. Starting in 1954 with support from Westinghouse, May Company offered its Freezer Food Service to any fridge-buying customer. A food consultant would assist the new fridge owner in selecting the amount and kind of food they required over six months. The consultant would order the food and make sure it would be delivered in a timely fashion.[103] This was a strange precursor to the monthly food subscription box like Blue Apron or Hello Fresh that many enjoy today.

May opened a new suburban location in November 1957 in the Cedar-Center Plaza at Cedar and Warrensville Roads in University Heights. This store became the locally famous "May's on the Heights." The building was designed by Victor Gruen Associates based in Detroit and Bialosky & Partners in Cleveland. It was a marvelous shopping experience vested with 346,000 square feet of a modern shopping mall store. The May's on the Heights also had a restaurant called the Mayfield Room and a Hough Bakery built right next to the restaurant. A beauty salon and full-service garage were built on the premises.

The company also constructed a nine-story warehouse (six stories tall with three sub-basements) that was attached to the south side of the Cedar Center store, originally designed to handle furniture distribution to Cleveland's east side suburbs. The red brick facility was designed to look like an integrated part of the store but essentially remained empty from 1960 until the University Heights store was demolished and rebuilt in 2002 as a rebranded Kaufman's.[104] The Heights store also had an auditorium.

To accommodate the significant increase in inventory and supplies, the May Company acquired a warehouse building in the Midtown area of Cleveland east of downtown. The large warehouse was located on East Forty-First Street and Payne Avenue, which occasionally opened to the public for special shopping events and was later used for clearance sales. At the time, it was widely considered to be one of the largest distribution centers in the country. The store also acquired the Tower Press Building to use as warehouse space but sold the facility before it was ever used for such a purpose.

The Taylor Son's department store, under the ownership of May Company, had opened a store at the Southgate Shopping Center in Maple Heights. The Taylor store had opened in 1958 but in April 1961 was converted into a May Company store. This branch store offered 204,000 square feet of retail space and two restaurants: The Tree-Top Room and the Bird Snack Bar. May Company decided to close the venerable Taylor Son & Company chain on December 17, 1961. The entire Taylor Son & Company inventory was transferred over to May, and a sizeable number of Taylor employees were then hired by May, too.

May Company announced a new branch store to be built in Parma. In August 1960, the store was opened in the Parmatown Mall. The branch store was 306,000 square feet and had only one restaurant, the Mayfair Room. The company had retained two architects—Victor Gruen of Los Angeles and Harry Sharpe of Cleveland—to design an eye-catching branch store. The building was constructed using reinforced concrete blocks with a textured brick façade and blue-and-white ceramic tiles providing accent. The building offered customers air conditioning and a central audio system. The building, when originally built, cost $7 million. It was demolished in 2014.

Continuity of its local management team was a big part of May's early success in the Cleveland market. Sam Rosenberg, who had worked at the downtown May store since 1933, announced his retirement in 1961. As general manager, Rosenberg had made great strides in expanding the May Company banner for downtown Cleveland to the fast-growing suburbs.

Rosenberg would daily walk across the street to Higbee's, where he would walk the floors and somehow get back into the stock rooms and docks to review his competitor's merchandise. Higbee employees were told to let him roam the store as he pleased. He died in 1977. Rosenberg was followed by Francis Coy, who held the general manager role for another ten years.

Following Coy, who retired in 1971, May named Denny G. Arvanites as the new leader of the growing May empire in Cleveland. Arvanites lasted a mere four years at the post and was succeeded by Raymond Klauer. Klauer himself lasted a few years, and was replaced by Gene Nau, who ran the Cleveland stores with vigor into the mid-1980s. Robert Cockayne replaced Nau in January 1984.

In 1963, May Company built two auto and tire centers at its branch locations. One was built at May's on the Heights and the other in Parmatown. The Great Lakes Mall store was opened in 1964 and was one of the smaller May Company stores in the region, providing 187,000 square feet of luxurious retail space. It had a restaurant also called the Mayfair Room; the restaurant had murals depicting the history of the Western Reserve of Ohio. The branch store offered multiple levels and featured open-air escalators. It was designed by famed architect Welton Becket Associates of Los Angeles. This store became a Kaufmann's in 1993.

May Company was the first local department store to issue its own personal charge card, announcing it on July 16, 1966, in a *Plain Dealer* article. It was time for May to break away from being part of the Department Stores Charge Plate (a metal card that was notched for each store and used at all participating members, which included Taylor Son & Company, Bailey's, Sterling Linder, Higbee's and Halle's).

To enhance the downtown shopping experience for its shoppers, the May Company announced in 1963 that it would build a three-thousand-car, nine-story parking garage on the site of the old Bailey's Department Store on Prospect Avenue immediately south of the May Company store. It was called the Parkade and was a self-service parking garage with an auto and tire center on the ground floor. Each floor of the parking garage had its own entrance into the May Company department store.

Additional May branch stores followed in the mid-1960s and 1970s as malls proliferated throughout northeast Ohio. These stores included Sheffield (formerly an O'Neil's and rebranded as May in 1964), Great Northern Mall (1965), Randall Park Mall (1976), Euclid Square Mall (1977) and Sandusky Mall (1979).

Bell in front of May's in the Heights, University Heights (1957).

The Great Northern branch store in North Olmsted was again designed by Welton Beckett Associates, which was becoming a favorite of the May Company management team in Cleveland. The store was 185,000 square feet in size over a three-story facility. The store offered a "unique Bermuda, spit-faced, precast stone exterior veneer featuring a highly decorative 17-foot chandelier."[105]

The May Company store in downtown Cleveland was listed in the National Register of Historic Places in 1974.[106] A party was held to commemorate this great honor. Expansive growth continued for the May Company in the Cleveland marketplace. In 1976, a new May store was opened in the Randall Park Mall complex. Randall Park was considered, at the time, the "largest Mall in the world." The mall was developed by shopping mall magnate Edward DeBartolo Sr. May hired RYA Architects of Dallas and Dalton, Dalton, Little & Newport of Cleveland to design the store. It was a sublime two-story structure with 177,000 available square feet of retail heaven.

The May Company specialized in the mid- to higher-end fashion merchandise and home furnishings. This target market placed May Company merchandise close to but usually slightly below its two major competitors in the Cleveland market, Halle's and Higbee's. The store was quite famous for its basement discount store, which sold seconds and closeouts from other stores as well as markdowns from the main selling floors.

May's also participated in the Green Eagle Stamp program. Trading stamps like the May Company Eagle Stamp got their start in department stores at the end of the nineteenth century. The first department store to champion the trading stamps was the Schuster's Department Store in Milwaukee. But the May Company's trading stamp program was one of the few proprietary stamp plans. Trading stamps were small paper stamps given to a customer by a retail store that acted similar to a loyalty card would today. The stamps were collected in stamp books and were redeemed for cash discounts on toys, housewares, clothing, furniture or appliances. Completed stamp books could be redeemed at any May Company store for three dollars in credits toward merchandise. The trading stamp program was administered by the May Company–owned Eagle Stamp Company based in St. Louis. The company existed from 1913 to 1987. The May Company in Cleveland started offering Eagle Stamps in 1908.

The retail landscape was beginning to radically change in the 1980s. With Reaganomics at full throttle and a seemingly endless supply of capital to finance any transaction, many beloved retail chains were

Early May Company delivery wagon (year not listed).

beginning to be acquired and merged into the operations of ever-larger holding companies. By 1983, the May Company enjoyed over $213 million in annual sales.[107]

In 1986, May Company acquired the Associated Dry Goods chain for $2.2 billion. It was the most expensive acquisition by May and one fueled mostly by debt. Associated was the fourth-largest retail conglomerate in the United States and operated a who's who of retail nameplates, including L.S. Ayers, Loehmann's, Lord & Taylor and J.W. Robinson's.[108] To generate some liquidity from the heavy burden of its debt holdings, May Company agreed in 1989 to sell half of its real estate holdings (mostly its retail real estate ownership). Part of these proceeds were used to pay down debt, while an additional $1.5 billion was used to acquire Filene's in Boston and Foley's in Houston.

May Company had built a cumbersome retail chain still using the now inefficient regional buyer and warehousing model implemented by its founder, David May, in the early 1900s. Financial engineering was going to be introduced into this model in order to find efficiencies and cost savings. Gone were regional buyers embedded in the stores and

Exterior view of May Company's new store at the Great Northern Shopping Center (1965).

local warehouses. These could be consolidated at the May Company headquarters in St. Louis.

In 1989, May Company merged its May Cleveland stores and its Akron-based O'Neil's stores to form a singular May Company Ohio. The May Company of Ohio was merged with Kaufmann's of Pittsburgh on October 17, 1992. The Kaufmann's nameplate won out, and all May Company stores became Kaufmann stores. For anyone following the interests of the Cleveland stores, it was a significant clue that big changes were coming to the May Company stores in Cleveland.

On January 31, 1993, the downtown Cleveland May Company store was closed. Despite bringing in over $19 million in revenue the year prior, the store was seen by many at Kauffman's as an expensive luxury that simply was not affordable anymore. Suburban stores would now be leading the operations at national retail chains. Downtown stores were not worth the trouble.

Troubled times were ahead for the company. In 1995, May Company sought the protection of federal bankruptcy. The company eventually cleared bankruptcy and began to consume more retail chains. In 2004, May Company acquired Marshall Fields, one of the iconic names in retailing, for $3.24 billion. On February 28, 2005, the Federated Department Stores announced that they would acquire the May Company for $11 billion.

By September 2006, all of the May regional nameplates, except for the venerable Lord & Taylor brand, ceased to exist.[109] All May company stores then became Macy's branded stores. Famous retail names like Marshall Field's, Filene's and Kaufman's simply disappeared. The last May Company operation in Ohio, a call center based in Lorain, was closed on July 1, 2006.

After many years nearly vacant, the downtown May Company building was swept up in the renaissance that Cleveland currently enjoys. Over the past few years, new skyscrapers have been built in downtown, as have numerous hotels and a brand-new convention center. Many old Cleveland buildings have enjoyed new life as apartment buildings. In 2017, the old May Company building was acquired by Bedrock-Detroit, a company controlled by Cleveland Cavaliers owner Dan Gilbert, for $12 million.[110] Bedrock-Detroit plans to build 308 apartments in the large complex. The redevelopment will also include 519 interior parking spaces. Through the course of the restoration, 200 terra-cotta stones will be replaced on the north elevation and over 1,100 on the south elevation.[111]

Bedrock-Detroit also acquired the Parkade built by the May Company in the 1960s (on the former Bailey Department Store site) that can offer an additional 670 parking spaces. This is not the first time Gilbert has renovated an old Cleveland department store. The old Higbee's building, in the Terminal Tower complex, was turned into a casino that he owns.

View of May Company's Mentor store located at the Great Lakes Mall (1964).

The Store

During its heyday, the downtown May Company store was rightly considered one of the great wonders of the retail world. It was refined, yet larger than life. It was a great world of discovery, want and desire. At its pinnacle of being a retail heavyweight, the downtown May Company store offered more than one million square feet of shopping paradise. When all the main construction was completed, May operated a large T-shaped complex with storefronts on Euclid Avenue, Ontario Street and Prospect Avenue.

The downtown store's directory might give insight into how rich its product offering was to its daily shoppers.

Basement
Malt Shop • May's Budget Store

First Floor
Gloves • Scarves • Handbags • Hosiery • Fashion Jewelry • Gold Standard • Fine Jewelry • Accessories • Slippers • Fragrances • Cosmetics • Notions • Blouses • Sweaters • Top Shop • Young Image • Boulevard Shoes • Career Shoes • Men's Accessories • Men's Furnishings • Men's Sportswear • Men's Fragrance Bar • A.C.E. • Luggage • Cameras

Prospect Level
Gourmet • Candy • Hough Bakeries • Eat 'n' Run • Stationery

Second Floor
Beauty Salon • Sleepwear • Foundations • Undershapers • Daywear • Leisurewear • Robes • Junior Intimates • Men's Slacks • Men's Outerwear • Men's Clothing • Men's Shoes • Quad Shop • Mike's Place • Quad Outerwear • Children's World • Girls' Accessories • Girls' 3–6X • Girls' 7–14 • Girls' Sleepwear • Boys' Shop • Cuddle Shop • Toddlers • Infants • Infants' Furniture • Children's Shoes

Third Floor
Young Ohioan Sportswear • Young Ohioan Dresses • Young Ohioan Shoes • Young Ohioan Coats • Misses Dresses • Social Occasion • Misses Moderate Separates • Misses Sportswear • Misses Coats • Career Dresses • Pavilion Dresses • Women's Sportswear • Women's Coats • Women's Dresses • Town and Country • Home and Town • Forecast Shop • Collections • Coat Salon •

The Ginger Snap • Contempo • Contempo Coats • Fur Salon • Shoe Salon • Contempo Shoes • Stagelight Makeup Center • Auditorium

Fourth Floor
Towels • Bath Shop • Domestics • Bedspreads • Draperies • Custom Fabrics • Fabrics • Art Needlework • Singer Sewing Center • Tabletop Shop • Cookie Corner • Trim-a-Home Shop • Music Center • Entertainment Center

Fifth Floor
Entertainment Center • Books • Hoffritz Cutlery • Fine Glassware • China • Silverware • Gift Isle • Housewares • Small Appliances • Cook's Pantry • Environments • Affordable Furniture • 3 Crowns Dining Room • Pub • Health and Beauty Aids

Sixth Floor
Furniture • Sleep Shop • Recliners • Sleep Sofas • Oriental Rug Gallery • Rugs • Carpeting • Religious Articles

Two women try on the latest style of shoes at the May Company store in downtown Cleveland (1931).

Seventh Floor

Entertainment Center • TVs • Stereos • Business Machines • Major Appliances • Dinettes • Sporting Goods • Toys • Garden Shop • Hardware • Customer Service

THE CHARACTERS

David May

May was the founder of one of the largest and most influential department store chains in the United States. He was born in 1848 into a Jewish family in the town of Kaiserlautern, then part of the Kingdom of Bavaria. The family immigrated to the United States in 1854 and originally settled in Cincinnati. He spent his teen years working in a clothing factory while attending Nelson College at night.

After living in Indiana for a few years, May moved to Colorado in 1878 for health reasons and settled in the small town of Leadville. A silver mining rush had turned the town into a bustling area. He eventually partnered with his soon-to-be brother-in-law Moses Shoenberg, and the two men opened a dry goods store to service the miners. In 1880, May married Rosa Shoenberg, and they eventually had four children together: Morton, Tom, Wilbur and Florene.

In 1887, May acquired another store, this time with his brothers-in-law Joseph and Louis Shoenberg (before the family changed its name to Beaumont) in Denver, Colorado. In 1892, May began his buying spree with the acquisition of the Famous Clothing Store in St. Louis, Missouri. He later acquired the famed Cleveland store that he renamed the May Company.

He famously built or acquired a retail chain that spanned from coast to coast. May acquired Bernheim-Leader (Baltimore), Kaufmann's (Pittsburgh), the Daniels & Fisher Stores (Denver), Hecht's (Baltimore), O'Neil's (Akron), Hamburger & Sons (Los Angeles), Fox & Company (Hartford) and Meier & Frank (Portland). He passed away at the age of seventy-nine in 1927 and was buried in St. Louis.

Shoppers inside the May Company building on Euclid Avenue (1965).

Nathan Dauby

Dauby was born on May 31, 1873, to parents David and Lena Dauby. At age fifteen, he started work at a shoe store as a clerk and two short years later became the store's manager. In 1892, Dauby opened the Dauby & Strauss shoe store with Emil Strauss. The store was famous for its one price for shoes. In 1898, Dauby bought out Strauss's shares. Dauby married Bessie in 1901, and they had a son, David, and daughter, Lucile.

In 1904, the May Company agreed to rent out its shoe department to Dauby. Shortly thereafter, he succeeded Commodore Beaumont as general manager of the store. He kept the general manager title at May Company Cleveland until 1945 and remained at the store until 1961.[112] He was a generous civic leader. He personally offered the largest gift to the Community Chest (now United Way) when the Cleveland chapter of the organization was founded.

It was Dauby who convinced the May Company to build a six-story building on Public Square in 1914. From 1945 until his death, he concentrated the majority of his time on philanthropic activities. Dauby worked on the Louis B. Beaumont Foundation. In 1952, he donated his mansion to the Cleveland Hearing and Speech Center. He died on May 17, 1964, leaving an estate worth $10 million with as much as $1.5 million allocated to local institutions.

Commodore Louis B. Beaumont

The brother-in-law of David May and co-founder of the May Company, the Commodore was a merchant, traveler, philanthropist and art connoisseur. Although he lived in Cleveland only eight years of his busy life, he was particularly fond of the city and enjoyed many close friendships there. He gave much of his time to the development of the May Company in Cleveland. He was succeeded by Nathan L. Dauby, under whose management the store became one of the largest in the nation.

His original last name was Schoenberg. Having a Jewish last name in pre–World War I Europe was challenging with the escalating racism and religious persecution, so he decided to change it to protect himself and his family. He spent a lot of time traveling between Cleveland, St. Louis and Europe. His foundation, the Louis B. Beaumont Foundation, was for many years a major force in Cleveland philanthropy.

Commodore Louis D. Beaumont died on October 1, 1942. He survived the three other co-founders of the May Department Stores Company and devoted the last thirty years of his life to travel, war service and personal supervision of the national memorial in honor of Wilbur Wright. Members of the American Expeditionary Force (AEF), involved in World

The May Company at Parmatown Shopping Center (1960).

Rendering of the May Company store scheduled for Euclid Square Mall. This store would comprise approximately 177,000 square feet on two separate levels.

The May Company store in the middle of the hustle and bustle at Public Square (year not listed). *Courtesy of Wetzler's Photography.*

War I, found free accommodations in French clubs through the generous contributions Beaumont made.[113]

It was announced on April 23, 1943, that bequests of the late Commodore totaled several million dollars, $565,000 of which was shared by eighteen Cleveland hospitals, educational and welfare institutions. The sum of $200,000 was designated for research by Western Reserve in memory of his son Dudley. Trustees of the fund were Nathan L. Dauby, vice president and general manager of the May Company; Morton J. May of St. Louis, president of the May Department Stores Company; and Nathan Loeser, Cleveland attorney and friend of the department store founder.

Nathan Loeser

Loeser was born in Cleveland to Moses and Marianna Loeser on August 8, 1869. Early in his life, the family moved to Buffalo. He studied law and journalism at Cornell University and, after graduating, worked as a writer for the *Buffalo Express*, *Buffalo Courier*, *New York Herald* and Associated Press. Loeser returned to Cleveland in 1892 and took a position in the law practice of Louis Grossman. He was admitted to the Bar Association four years later. In 1920, Loeser established Mooney, Hahn, Loeser & Keogh, now Hahn Loeser. He did significant legal work for the May Company and Bailey's Department Store as well. Loeser was keenly involved in the affairs and growth of the Mount Sinai Hospital in Cleveland. He passed away on June 30, 1953.

STERLING LINDER DAVIS DEPARTMENT STORE

Homemaker's Headquarters

The History

The Sterling Linder Davis Department store story is a fascinating and complex tale of multiple once vibrant department stores coming together out of financial necessity but failing to become one of Cleveland's largest and most successful retail chains. The company was a combination of three smaller retail stores: the Sterling & Welch Company, the W.B. Davis Company and the Linder Company. Each store had a unique niche to which it catered. Yet combined, they created an almost mythological brand in the minds of many Clevelanders. Sterling specialized in home furnishings; Davis pioneered menswear. And Linder's was famous for being the largest women's fashion store in Cleveland. Mostly known today as the store with the largest decorated Christmas tree display in Ohio, Sterling Linder Davis was an iconic Cleveland retailer revered for its opulence and luxury.

The Store

The Sterling & Welch Company

The Sterling store can trace its lineage back to the Beckwith Dry Goods Company, which was founded by Thomas and William Beckwith in 1845.

The chain started with a humble storefront on Superior Avenue. For years, the store offered the basic necessities for its patrons, but in 1857, it replaced its dry goods with floor coverings and curtains.[114] As Beckwith aged, it presented an opportunity for two of its employees to buy into the business—Frederick Sterling and George Welch. The pioneering retail store moved to Euclid Avenue in 1874, taking over the Central Rink on the south side of the square. With growth came the need for a new location, and in 1893, the aspiring entrepreneurs moved the store to 10 Euclid Avenue. It was a magnificent store with rather ornate lighting, new glass displays and thick, soft carpeting to give the store a luxurious appearance. By 1899, the two men had established a controlling interest in the retail store and by 1902 had incorporated and renamed the store the Sterling & Welch Company.

The company catered heavily to its Millionaires' Row clientele, especially the housewives of the great industrialists. While the foot traffic was sublime and large profits were made, the two gentlemen soon decided that they needed a new store to offer more merchandise, especially housewares and furnishings. It was resolved in 1909 to move the company from its lower Euclid Avenue perch to a more refined upper Euclid Avenue location.

The news was out—Cleveland's pioneer carpet and interior-decoration house, the Sterling & Welch Company, ventured to upper Euclid Avenue to a permanent location, 1225 Euclid, which the company acquired from James J. Tracy. Tracy would be called a real estate speculator today. He started off in banking working for the Commercial Bank but slowly started to acquire real estate in the downtown Cleveland area. Over time, he acquired substantial property, including business blocks in the heart of the city. He was also an original member of the "Arkites."[115] An Arkite was one who was a member of the Ark, an informal gathering place for the early Cleveland intelligentsia, which led to the establishment of many of the city's cultural institutions, especially the Cleveland Museum of Natural History.[116] But the 1225 Euclid Avenue location has a deeper past.

Originally, the plot was the home of Amasa Stone, a successful railroad entrepreneur and civic leader of Cleveland. It was built in 1857. He constructed a 6,500-square-foot Italianate villa. Stone was one of the wealthy elites who built their amazing, egregious homes along Euclid Avenue. In 1875, a railroad that Stone had constructed over the Ashtabula Gorge collapsed, killing 151 train passengers and crew. Stone could not contain his remorse and, feeling the burden of the disaster, failing health, the drowning

The Linder Davis (precursor of the Sterling Linder Davis department store) is getting a modernized exterior and interior. Sterling Welch department store is in the foreground (1949).

of his son and the pinch of a financial panic, committed suicide at the home while in his bathtub. He placed a gun to his heart and pulled the trigger. After his death, one of his daughters, Flora Stone Mather, and her husband, Samuel Mather, lived in the home until she died in 1909. The manse was bought by Tracy and then sold. On the land, both Sterling & Welch and Higbee's built new department stores.

Sterling & Welch was "the store" for Cleveland's wealthy elite. The store began to receive high praise from national newspapers and trade magazines as one of Ohio's finest and largest home furnishing stores. Hopes were high that the new store would reinforce the glamour Sterling & Welch stood for in the Sixth City. The department store retained architect J. Milton Dyer, and construction began in earnest on a five-story steel structure, located at 1225–39 Euclid Avenue, with a magnificent terra-cotta exterior. The building is believed to have cost an astounding $500,000 to complete.

Dyer was an inspired selection as the architect. Born in Pennsylvania, at age eleven his family moved to Cleveland. They settled into the "Rock's Corner" area of East Fifty-Fifth Street and Woodland Avenue. After graduating from Case Institute of Technology, he studied architecture at the École Nationale Superieure des Beaux-Arts in Paris. He took a role at the Warner & Swasey company. He rubbed elbows with other prominent architects of the day—Frank Walker and Henry Weeks, to name a couple.

But it was his architectural flair that still resonates in Cleveland today. His influence on the modern Cleveland we witness today is undeniable. He designed the Republic Oil Company building, Taylor's Department Store and its arcade, the Swasey Observatory (located in East Cleveland), the Tavern Club (he was also a member), the Cleveland Athletic Club (renovated as an upscale apartment building), the Cleveland Coast Guard Station, Cleveland Music Settlement School and Cleveland City Hall. His work on the Spirit of Progress exposition in 1909 is still considered legendary. Unfortunately, some of his masterpieces were torn down. Especially noteworthy were the Central National Bank building, First National Bank building, Guardian Trust building and the Peerless Motor Car factory.

Dyer, as an adult, lived with his mother in his homestead on East Seventy-First Street until she died in 1923. His sister then moved in, and he lived with her until she, too, passed in 1954. He died in 1957 and is buried in Woodland Cemetery.[117]

The store opened in May 1909 and was the fourth-largest department store in Cleveland. It was an architectural gem that doubled as a luxurious department store immediately installing awe in anyone who walked through the doors. Sterling Welch's legendary French-style wrought-iron and glass-front portico was a welcome sight for shoppers ready to see the newest thing in luxury goods and to spend their money. As noted by early Cleveland historian Samuel Peter Orth:

> *It is undoubtedly the finest, most commodious and handsomest store building in the world, it being unsurpassed by any in Chicago, New York or the metropolitan centers of Europe. It is strictly modern in every sense, with magnificent interior furnishings and every facility to promote the beauty and substantiality of the structure.*[118]

The company invested heavily in its advertising as well—a necessity in the competitive Cleveland retail market at the time. The W.N. Gates Company handled the Sterling & Welch advertising portfolio for many years. The Gates Company was founded by William Nahum Gates, who

The famed Sterling Linder Christmas tree (1940).

opened his original advertising business on Public Square where the Hotel Cleveland (now the Renaissance) rests today. The Gates business then moved to the Keith Building in later years; it was considered the second-oldest advertising company in the United States, superseded by the Ayer & Son agency in Philadelphia.[119]

Over the years, further advancements were made in the company's product portfolio, including lighting, refrigerators, irons and washing machines—all high-end, high-value products. In the 1920s, Sterling Welch vastly improved its delivery fleet, allowing delivery directly to the shoppers' homes. The store was the first to introduce an art gallery for patrons seeking expensive art to adorn their precious walls. A famous artist known as "Cleveland's first impressionist painter," Lydia May Ames was the featured artist selected for the inaugural gallery exhibit in the fifth-floor gallery of the famed store. Ames also exhibited in New York, Philadelphia, Buffalo, Detroit and Mansfield, Ohio. She passed away in 1946, but for the last twenty years of her life, Ames operated her own studio, where she continued to teach classes. Ames lived on Miles Avenue, and scenes from nearby Garfield Park were one of her favorite subjects.[120]

In 1929, the store—given the economic circumstances—opened its own bargain basement liquidation area. During the Great Depression, the store tended to help its clientele with special financing options. The famous Sterling Christmas tree was unveiled in the store's atrium in 1927. Management of the store invested heavily in mail-order shopping and special mail-in coupons. Arthur V. Hook, an official for thirty-four years at the company, became president in 1944 when F.A. Sterling died.[121]

By the late 1940s, however, the store was beginning to feel the pinch of the post–World War II consumer due to changing tastes. Perhaps, Sterling clung too long in offering classic designed furniture, clothing and accessories. Quite frankly, after World War II, Sterling Welch was considered "stodgy." Changes needed to be made at this classic department store. And a dramatic turn for Sterling Welch was nigh.

The W.B. Davis Company

Eager entrepreneurs William Davis and Edwin Parsons pooled their resources together and started one of Cleveland's first and finest men's haberdasheries. The store started in 1879 as a custom shirt maker, and a year later, Davis began to offer men's furnishings. On the top floor of a three-story building at the corner of Superior Avenue and Bank Street, Davis and Parsons opened their custom shirt factory. Two years later, they secured a ground-floor location for a men's furnishings store on the north side of Superior Street between Seneca and Public Square.

Employees strike at Sterling Welch (1946).

The Davis men's store was located on the corner of Superior Avenue and Bank Street (now West Sixth Street). Sales were strong at this location, so Davis decided he needed to move to a larger store, and in 1896, the company moved to a more prestigious location at 21 Euclid Avenue. It was not that far from the original Sterling Welch store—simply a hop, skip and a jump away. Davis made a financially fateful decision in 1900 when he won the rights to the Aertex brand for men's sports apparel, particularly workout undergarments. This was a huge success that fed into his focus on men's apparel and fashions.

In 1907, given the continued success of the Davis brand, another, larger location was required, and it was soon settled that a new Davis store would open at 311 Euclid Avenue next to the Old Arcade. Here, given the expansive new floor plan, Davis could begin to offer women's and children's fashion lines. Davis opened a small discount store on Superior Avenue to sell any overstocked items, and he began to rent additional floors at the Euclid Avenue location.

A keen businessman and fantastic promoter of the Davis brand, William Davis enjoyed advertising to his clientele. In 1916, Davis Company produced a little guide for men on how to best pick fashions and styles. The book was titled *Correct Dress*. In addition, Davis implemented new credit and return policies.

The store enjoyed great success, and by 1917, yet a larger store was needed. That year, the company moved from its earlier location on Euclid Avenue to the newly acquired Davis Building at 325 Euclid Avenue. Not forgetting its roots as a men's haberdashery, the company announced in 1918 that it would carry the Kuppenheimer clothing line and would be Cleveland's exclusive Hickey-Freeman retail partner. Presidents Garfield, McKinley and Harding shopped with Davis, as did John D. Rockefeller. Davis also founded the Davis Laundry & Cleaning Company.

To keep with changing tastes in the 1920s, the company opened up a hair salon and a restaurant, Schuder's. The store also opened a unique golf department that took advantage of the national golfing fervor. Davis retired from the store in 1927 but continued to be a voice of reason to management over the next fourteen years. The Depression years were not kind to the Davis Company, and while sales seemed to improve in the early 1940s, the department store never quite had the same cache as before. Davis died in 1941 and was remembered, appropriately, as a retail innovator and titan of Cleveland's department stores. But his death took its toll on the spirit of the store. After many years fighting rumor and innuendo, the Davis store was sold to Allied Stores in late 1947 for the paltry price of $750,000.

The Linder Company

The Linder Company was formed in April 1908 and opened its initial retail shop on East Ninth Street in part of the premises later occupied by the Cleveland Trust Company. The store was started by Max Linder, Max Hellman and Morris Black. (In the file-this-under-it's-a-small-world category, the co-founder of the company, Max Linder, was the grandfather of musician and wife of a former Beatle Linda McCartney.)[122] Linder focused on the finest women's fashion, especially high-end goods from Paris.

The namesake of the department store, Max Linder, moved to Cleveland a number of years prior to launching the Linder Company. He came to Cleveland to serve as the general manager of a New York

City branch store called Oppenheim Collins that was located on East Ninth Street. Oppenheim specialized in women's clothing and fashions and was a retail fixture in Cleveland until it closed in 1930. He stayed at Linder Company until 1920, when he decided to become a merchandise buyer for the May Company. Max passed away in 1945 at the age of seventy-three. Hellman, too, was established in the women's fashion industry and served as president of Linder Company until his untimely passing at forty-seven years of age in 1923. Morris Black then became president of the toney department store and served in that capacity until he passed away in 1938.

Their focus on upscale women's fashion was a hit with the upper crust of Cleveland society. Linder's modest East Ninth Street store could not accommodate its growth, and a decision was made to build a unique retail store in the upper Euclid Avenue area where a number of other department stores had moved. Funds were appropriated to buy some land near Playhouse Square.

In 1915, the company decided to move to 1331 Euclid Avenue. The Lindner Building was one of the major works of progressive architect Robert Kohn. Kohn was based out of New York City and was well known for designing the Old New York Evening Post and Spero Buildings in Manhattan. He also had designed the Tower Press Building in Cleveland located on Superior Avenue. That building was built in 1907 and is legendary for its 130-foot octagonal tower at its core. The Tower Press Building is now an apartment building complex.

The Linder building is an important Cleveland landmark. Its open glass façade and its combination of Classical and Art Nouveau motifs were a departure from the commercial styles of the era and remain a unique asset to the city. The building was purchased and remodeled by the New York–based Bonwit Teller Company in the late 1940s.[123] After Bonwit left, the building became a discount store, Gen Mart, in the 1970s and then became vacant. The Linder Building is now home to United Way and is called the Mandel Community Building.

The building boasted new amenities for its shoppers, including a millinery and a popular tearoom. Expansion beckoned, and by the late 1920s, there were Linder Company stores in Toledo and Mansfield, Ohio; Erie, Pennsylvania; and Elmira and Binghamton, New York. The Depression had left its effects on Linder, but the chain weathered the times better than most. The store used new installment payment plans and ran various sales to build traffic. The women's-only chain made a unique decision during the Depression to add some men's lines, including dress ties, Oxford shirts, men's suits, sports jackets and dress slacks. It was a radical departure from the very successful focus on women. Also, the company copied other department stores by adding a new restaurant to its operations. The Continental successfully opened in 1936 and served French cuisine.

The early 1940s were great times for the Linder Company. Executives of the company were Mack Gordon, president, and Simon Olson, vice president. But the expansive days of the war years fell prey to a modest recession in 1946, and the store was losing money. In 1947, Allied Department Stores acquired Linder Company and merged it with the W.B. Davis Company—sure to be a Cleveland-based retail powerhouse.

Allied bought Linder for $1 million. Soon after the sale of Linder's, an announcement was made by Bonwit Teller that it was set to occupy the famed Linder Building. The new Linder-Davis department store was going to move to the old Higbee's store located on the northwest corner of Euclid Avenue and East Thirteenth Street, right next door to Sterling & Welch. Allied Stores at the time was a successor to the Hahn Department Store and was operating a large number of Jordan Marsh stores when it acquired Linder & Davis.

The purchase was so successful that Allied decided to acquire the Sterling & Welch operation as well. In August 1949, the Linder & Davis department store opened in the remodeled Higbee Building adjacent to the Sterling & Welch store. The following year, the two companies were merged into Sterling Linder Davis until 1958, when Davis was dropped from the marquee. The new Sterling Linder store launched a popular travel agency, Allen Travel Agency, and promoted the Red Hat Service. This service was offered to busy businessmen who didn't have time to shop but wanted the "perfect gift" for their wives. Parisian fashion shows were popular annual events. Allied felt that with this new retail powerhouse in downtown Cleveland no suburban stores were necessary. This proved to be a disastrous long-term decision for Sterling Linder.

Sterling Linder's Christmas tree event was becoming an iconic event for Clevelanders. The store's Christmas tree was the stuff of legends. The tradition was started in the Sterling & Welch store in 1927, and by 1952, the store boasted the following: "A live 50 foot tree, festooned with 60 pounds of 'icicles,' 1,000 pounds of tinsel, 1500 ornaments and illuminated by six banks of 750-candle watt spotlights. It requires 650 man hours to trim by swinging stages suspended by the skylight."

The store's Santaland exhibit included a device where you could insert a coin and receive a gift. Sterling Linder created the "Aisle of Gifts" for the male shopper. The aisle was placed in the store's vast atrium, making Christmas shopping vastly easier for men.[124] The store also promoted Lindee the Easter Bunny in the spring. Every Christmas season, local ice cream fountain Sweet Moses, located in Cleveland's now developed Detroit Shoreway neighborhood, celebrates Sterling Linder during the holidays with the Sterling Linder sundae. The treat includes peppermint stick ice cream, hot fudge, whipped cream and a special Christmas cookie.

In 1954, the department store was the first in the Cleveland area to offer colored TVs. The 1950s were seen as the golden era for Sterling Linder. In 1956, the Equitable Life Assurance Society, so enamored of the growth prospects of the store, invested $3 million in the brand. A new parking lot was planned to be built on the site of the store's former warehouse (East Twelfth Street and Chester Avenue). Other groups displaced by this massive construction included the Navy Building, WEWS-TV, Innerman's Records, Evangel Book and the International

Children riding an indoor carousel at Sterling Linder department store (1949).

Shop.[125] The lot was ready by 1957. Even with parking adjacent to the store, Sterling Linder offered a free shuttle from Terminal Tower to its location farther up on Euclid Avenue.

By the early 1960s, it was becoming evident that the Sterling Linder brand could not survive with a single downtown Cleveland flagship store. But Allied had little appetite for expanding the brand to suburban areas. Multiple strategies were bandied about the boardroom, including turning the once luxurious retailer into a discount chain, changing up the brand's image and design or outright closing the store. Other retail chains were approached to buy Sterling Linder, but all refused.

The City of Cleveland understood the changing dynamics of its downtown area and hired I.M. Pei to design a new look for the fatigued northeast quadrant of downtown Cleveland. The goal was to use federal funds to tear down hundreds of tired structures and buildings and invest in new infrastructure and downtown development. In 1963, a Boston-based developer and the City of Cleveland agreed to apply eminent

Two ladies drinking tea at the Sterling Welch department store (1928).

The Sterling-Linder warehouse located at East Twelfth Street and Chester Avenue (1964).

domain on Sterling Linder's parking area (and former warehouse) for a new apartment development called the Chesterfield Apartments. Allied agreed to sell the lot for $3.2 million, but the city was only willing to pay $1.6 million. The parties went to court to settle their financial differences, and the city won.

This loss accelerated Allied's decision to leave the Cleveland marketplace. On July 9, 1968, Allied announced the closing of Sterling Linder, and over one hundred years of retail excellence was lost. Soon thereafter, a real estate developer promised a new modern building for the site. Midwestern Land Development Corporation purchased the Sterling Linder building. The plan was to build a new four-hundred-unit hotel on the west parcel of the property. That part of the Sterling Linder building was torn down, but the hotel never materialized, and the original Sterling building was then used as a parking lot. A bank was placed at the street level of the building, and offices were constructed on the upper floors.

The fur salon at the Sterling Linder Davis department store (1949).

The remaining structure is now home to some tech companies, including BlueBridge Networks, which has its name on the façade. For a period of time, Lone Star Funds owned the building after it had gone into foreclosure from a previous owner. A new Cleveland-based ownership group bought the building from Lone Star Funds for $7.1 million.[126]

The immediate closing of Sterling Linder by Allied Department Stores had little effect on Allied's performance. In the early 1980s, Allied acquired a retail conglomerate that included Brooks Brothers, Garfinkel's and Miller & Rhoads. These acquisitions stressed the financial condition of Allied. Eventually, Allied and another prime national retailer, Federated, were combined in a failed merger by Canadian business maverick Robert Campeau. Four years later, the chain entered bankruptcy. In 1992, the company emerged from bankruptcy as Federated Department Stores with Macy's now as its banner department store brand.

The Characters

Frederick A. Sterling

Frederick Augustine Sterling was born in Salisbury, Connecticut, a son of Frederick and Caroline M. (Dutcher) Sterling. The Sterling family came to this country from England in the seventeenth century and first settled in Lyme, Connecticut. The elder Frederick Sterling owned an iron foundry at Salisbury, Connecticut, prior to moving to Cleveland, where he turned his attention to the business of handling hardwood and furnishing ties and other materials to service the railroad companies.

The younger Sterling became a resident of Cleveland at the age of eighteen and took a position with Wick & Beckwith. Soon afterward, Mr. Wick retired, and the firm was renamed T.S. Beckwith & Company. Sterling became a partner at the age of twenty-one. In 1864, the firm name was changed to Beckwith & Sterling, and in 1874, it moved from Superior Street to Euclid Avenue. Upon the death of Beckwith in 1876, the firm name was again changed to Sterling & Company. Later, with Mr. Welch coming into the firm, it became known as the Sterling & Welch Company.

Sterling was a director of the Citizens Saving & Trust Company, the Union National Bank, the Kelley Island Line & Transportation Company and Columbia Gas & Electric Company. He married Emma Betts, of Meadville, Pennsylvania, whose father was one of the early settlers of the western portion of the Keystone State. They had one son, Willis Betts Sterling, who graduated from Yale College and the Columbia Law School. Sterling was a member of the Union Club, the Country Club and, for a period of time, president of the board of trustees of the Second Presbyterian Church.

Morris Black

Morris Black, born in 1868, was an influential businessman and civic leader of Cleveland. He was born in Toledo to Hungarian Jewish immigrants, and the family moved to Cleveland in 1892. Black eventually graduated from Harvard University and joined his father's business, the H. Black Company, a manufacturer of women's Wooltex coats and suits. H. Black Company was one of the largest manufacturers of women's clothing in the United States. The company was located on Superior

Avenue in what is now called the Tower Press Building. The firm specialized in fine fabrics and ready-to-wear clothing that was marketed under the Wooltex brand.[127]

Black became president of the Linder Company in 1913 and stayed in that role until 1936. For the next two years, he worked as a business consultant until he died in 1938. He was instrumental in forming the Civic League and chaired the City Plan Commission from 1915 to 1925. He also served for a time as the president of the chamber of commerce.[128]

WILLIAM TAYLOR SON & COMPANY

Honesty in Word & Ware

THE HISTORY

Somewhere in the crowded immigrant streets of Boston were two bold and cunning Scotsmen with big dreams in their heads and holes in their pockets. They came to America with everything they owned in satchels and sacks with the hope that they—someday—would own their own little store. Their own little slice of America. But today that dream would have to wait; William Taylor and Thomas Kilpatrick needed money. And in order to get money, they needed work, desperately. Both men ended up working at Hogg, Brown & Taylor in Boston. At the time, Hogg, Brown & Taylor was the largest dry goods store in the United States—bigger than any retail store in New York. One of the proprietors at the retail store, it turns out, was William's older brother.

The two enterprising lads had heard whispers of this boomtown out by the Great Lakes named Cleveland. It was the land of milk and honey. The stories were so good and unbelievable that they had to be true, and so they left for Cleveland in late 1869. On April 21, 1870, they opened a dry goods store called Taylor & Kilpatrick. They were lucky to find some good space for their business on the south side of Euclid Avenue just east of Public Square. The original Taylor store occupied the first floor of the Cushing Block on Euclid. Their neighbor upstairs in the building was a small upstart named the Standard Oil Company, managed by a gentleman named John D. Rockefeller.

Men unloading boxes from a plane into a Taylor Company van (1945).

Contrary to advice that the Cushing Block would be an unfortunate commercial location, the store, staffed with thirty-six salesmen, prospered. Thus began the retailing trend away from Superior Avenue to Euclid. The store was fitted with ten large chandeliers that blazed on certain evenings when Taylor's was open until ten o'clock. "One price for all" was the pioneering principle introduced to the trade by William Taylor. He was a devout Presbyterian who insisted on strict Sunday observance; traditionally, the store did not advertise on Sundays, and curtains on the show windows were drawn until 1939.

The site of the original Taylor & Kilpatrick store has a fascinating story. The plot was owned by Judge Samuel Cowles, a Cleveland pioneer. In 1842, his widow sold their home on Euclid Street (the original Taylor store site), with land running all the way to Prospect, for $7,000. Fast-forward to 1915, and the same property was valued at $6,000 per foot front or roughly $900,000 for the full lot. Space was selling for a premium in the growing city. In any case, Judge Cowles was a pioneering lawyer and real estate investor in Cleveland. Originally from Simbury, Connecticut,

Cowles moved to Cleveland in 1818. He was a partner in two different law firms while alive. He specialized in real estate transactions as a lawyer. He acquired extensive landholdings and was one of the early settlers who profited from Cleveland's growth.

Before the arrival of the Taylor store, Bishop Amadeus Rappe invited the Ursuline Sisters of France to establish a select academy for girls in Cleveland in 1850. Rappe had acquired the former Judge Samuel Cowles home on Euclid Street and intended to have the academy open in September. A charter was granted to Ursuline College for Women in 1871. The school was moved to the west side of Scovill Avenue at Wilson Avenue in 1893, and it remained as the Mother House for the Sisters even after the college was established on Overlook Road in the late 1920s.

Rappe himself is an interesting character in Cleveland history. He was the first bishop of the Diocese of Cleveland. Born in Audrehem, France, he studied at the College of Boulogne-sur-Mer and the seminary at Arras. He was ordained in 1829. Rappe was recruited by Bishop John Purcell to come to Ohio.[129] Initially, he was the pastor of the St. Francis Parish in Toledo. On April 23, 1847, Pope Pius IX established the new Diocese of Cleveland, and Rappe was consecrated as the bishop of the new diocese in October of that same year. Rappe immersed himself in the construction of St. John Cathedral and actively recruited European priests and nuns to America. He was instrumental in opening the first general hospital in Cleveland, St. Vincent Charity Hospital. So much history in one little plot of Cleveland dirt.

Taylor & Kilpatrick slowly built up their clientele and added new products and services when time and money allowed. Every year witnessed an enlargement of the retail floor space. Both Taylor & Kilpatrick had the knack for innovating within their business. The store held late hours, which was an unheard-of amenity for after-work shoppers. Taylor & Kilpatrick offered mail-in orders and, much later, customer service phone numbers. Their best "gimmick" was to forego the traditional bartering technique used between shopper and shop owner and simply list non-negotiable price tags on all their wares.

Kilpatrick decided to retire from the retail business in 1886. Taylor assumed control of the business and, in a fit of great confidence, opened a second store in downtown, which was mainly used as a wholesale outlet while the original store maintained its retail store aura. Taylor's son John Livingston Taylor joined the company in 1887, and the store was renamed William Taylor Son & Company. Tragically, his son's involvement with the company was a short tenure, as John died a young man in 1892.

Taylor Department Store escalator being turned on while a crowd of shoppers looks on (1946).

The immediate dilemma with John's passing and William's desire to retire was who was going to run the company. After a lot of personal reflection, William came to the conclusion that his daughter-in-law was the best person to lead the store into the next century. It was, at the time, a shocking decision (few women were put in charge of a growing enterprise) but the right one. Sophia Strong Taylor had grown up in a professional service company and had learned a lot of the business world being at the hip of her father. She took the reins of the Taylor Son & Company in 1892 and did not relinquish control until 1935, when she somewhat reluctantly turned it over to her brother Colonel Charles Strong. She died the year after stepping down.

Taylor's fortunes grew with the city's fortunes. As hundreds of thousands of new immigrants came to Cleveland, the store became a trusted resource. But with growth came concerns of construction. The company needed a new, larger building to manage its sales growth. Sophia convinced the board of directors to approve the construction of a new building, and a sizeable plot was acquired on Euclid Avenue to build a full-service department store.

In 1907, William Taylor Son & Company constructed a five-story, terra cotta–clad building that employed nearly two thousand people. The building was located at 630 Euclid Avenue (now listed as 668 Euclid Avenue). The Taylor Arcade opened in 1907 in conjunction with the opening of the new Taylor store. The arcade ran between Euclid Avenue and Prospect Avenue, just west of the Taylor department store and east of the Euclid and Colonial arcades, also on Euclid Avenue. John Rust had built the original Euclid Arcade in 1892, and it proved so popular that the Colonial and Taylor arcades followed. While the department store always owned the arcade, at first it rented out retail space to over forty different shop owners. However, in the 1930s, the store expanded and took over the space for its own use.[130]

In 1913, the store decided to add four new floors as the department store continued to experience revenue growth. Plans were drawn up to replace this building with a twenty-story department store building in 1927. The Great Depression gave pause to building anything larger.

The 1927 expansion would have been a game-changer for Taylor Son & Company, as well as Cleveland. It was in a set of brilliant renderings for this unbuilt project that Walker & Weeks's efforts on the tall commercial building reached a climax. The existing Taylor store at 630 Euclid Avenue was already the product of several stages of building by Walker & Weeks. A large expansion was planned, and drawings were made for a building on the same site. The perspective drawings by Wilbur H. Adams, one of the men who produced most of the Walker & Weeks renderings, showed a building filling the entire block between Euclid and Prospect and culminating in

Taylor Southgate store exterior (1961).

Elevator operators for William Taylor Department Store in downtown Cleveland (1961).

a vast tower. The renderings emphasized sculptural mass and shape in great building blocks rather than architectural detail. Likewise, the Taylor store renderings do not show enough detail even to indicate the number of stories; the surroundings suggest there may have been between twenty and twenty-five. The great mass of the Taylor store building steps up in four dramatic stages in a complex series of ziggurat-like setbacks. The project was greatly reduced in scope by the onset of the Depression, but had it been built, the Taylor store would have rivaled parts of the Terminal Tower complex in its effect on Cleveland's skyline.[131]

The store quickly gained a reputation, at this new location, as being one of the finest retailers in the world and often drew comparisons to Harrod's and Selfridge's in London. This was due to Taylor's elaborate architectural design, which reminded world travelers of the similarity to the chic British retailers. Taylor also stocked a wide selection of British merchandise.

Taylor Son & Company was once at the forefront of technology as well. The company invested heavily in radio photography to gain a competitive advantage over its retail peers. This technology allowed the sending of new fashions from Europe to be transferred to the United States within eight hours. Western Union (originally a Cleveland-based company founded by Jeptha Wade) transmitted its first radio photo in 1921. RCA followed in 1926. Taylor Son & Company could show Clevelanders new fashion trends well before any of its rivals.

In the 1930s, Taylor Son & Company continued to expand by acquiring the adjacent Taylor Arcade and the Clarence Building, which were then incorporated into the ever-expanding floor plan of the store. During the Great Depression, Taylor was lucky to survive, as many local and regional chains did not. Taylor & Son survived by cutting staff and prices, not to mention running a lot of sales and promotions. In 1934, the retail store embarked upon a significant remodeling plan for the Euclid Avenue store. The $500,000 improvement included new bronze light fixtures throughout the store, new overhead lighting systems, faster elevators and larger department floor plans.[132]

Sophia Taylor—the strong matriarch and savior of the store—quietly passed away in September 1936. After Sophia's passing, ownership control of William Taylor Son & Company went to her brother, Major Charles H. Strong. He had assumed operational control a year earlier. Strong immediately stopped the sixty-nine-year-old custom: the store's display windows were opened to public view on the Sabbath, and a policy of advertising in Sunday papers was inaugurated.

In 1931, Strong married Eleanor Painter, a grand star of the theater and opera. She took an active interest in the Musical Arts Association and participated in Cleveland's important musical activities. Painter appeared with the Cleveland Orchestra on several occasions in artistic readings and devoted some time to writing about music. She was an extraordinary beauty. Painter had been previously married but was smitten with Strong.

Painter had grown up in Colorado and later moved to New York City to pursue a singing career. By 1912, she was studying singing in Berlin, Germany, and debuted at Covent Garden in London the following year. She sang for five seasons with the Charlottenburg Opera in Berlin and, between seasons in 1914, starred in *The Lilac Domino* in New York City. Composer Victor Herbert wrote the operetta *The Princess Pat* for her. She had won international fame as a prima donna. Painter lived in Cleveland with Strong until he died on November 3, 1947.

After Charles Strong took controlling interest in the company, he remade the board of directors by inviting Edgar Hahn and William Kenough to join him. Soon after Sophia's passing, Charles was approached by the May Company. Charles could see the macro events happening with the retail sector, and he knew that if he didn't have partners with access to larger pools of capital, then Taylor Son & Company would remain a single-store company. Strong managed the Taylor operations until 1945, when the ownership structure of the store, which included May Company, was made public. May Company then took over day-to-day operations.

So, in 1939, the May Company took a minority position in Taylor's despite the fact that May owned the largest department store in Ohio, no more than two blocks away on Euclid Avenue. May had exercised a similar transaction with the O'Neil's Department Store in Akron, Ohio. As part of the investment in Taylor Son & Company, May requested that Charles Strong step down as president. David Scholl succeeded Strong and stayed on as president of the company until 1960. May continued to make equity investments in Taylor throughout the 1940s. This favorable move by May Company enabled May to expand its retail reach beyond its traditional upper-middle-class base to service the working-class folks who shopped at Taylor's.[133] In 1945, May approved and completed a $2 million expansion in the Taylor's Euclid Avenue store. It was at this time that the May Company ownership of Taylor Son & Company was initially acknowledged publicly.

The William Taylor Department Store arcade within the downtown Cleveland store on Euclid Avenue (1945).

This public announcement had its effects on the retail chain. During the 1920s, Taylor's was asked to become a member of the Associated Merchandising Company, a merchandising and industry research collaborative. The store was selected by other members of the AMC. Taylor's maintained its membership in the AMC, giving it a major pricing advantage over its retail peers, until 1946, when Higbee's was asked to take Taylor's membership in the collective. Neither Taylor nor May had publicly acknowledged the question of ownership until 1945. Now its pricing advantage was gone.

Despite this, the partnership served both companies well. May had access to a whole new group of shoppers. Taylor found a solid financial partner that could help it grow its operations. Further investments continued. In 1959, Taylor Son & Company asked for additional financial support to invest in a $1.5 million air conditioning system in a store now fifty years old. The downtown store received a modest update in 1960, with new display windows and outside lighting. Around this time, the store built a car garage on Huron Road with access to the Prospect Avenue entrance.

The Hippodrome Theater and the Taylor Department Store on Euclid Avenue (1961).

Free bus to Taylor's. The bus took passengers from Terminal Tower to the Taylor Department Store on Euclid Avenue to Playhouse Square and back again (1955).

In 1958, Taylor's built a branch unit in Maple Heights, Ohio, at the Southgate Shopping Center. Real estate developer Ernest Siegler opened the Southgate Shopping Center in 1955 and was seeking a large department store to anchor the retail center. This new store cost Taylor Son & Company and May Company nearly $5 million and was considered a stunning architectural gem with gray bricks, concrete, large glass windows and white canyon stone. Designed by the Los Angeles–based architecture firm of Welton Beckett Associates, it was a powerful architectural statement by Taylor Son & Company—three stories and 204,000 square feet of iconic retail space, including the Tree Top Restaurant and the Jiffy Bird Snack Bar. It was rebranded a May Company store in 1961 and remained a May branded store until 1989, when it was unfortunately demolished.

There were a number of macro events that were threating the existence of Taylor Son & Company at this time. First, the late 1950s and early '60s experienced economic tumult with nearly back-to-back recessions.

The new four-hundred-car parking garage of Taylor Department Store (1958).

Taylor Department Store Christmas display (1958).

It should be noted that over forty U.S. department store chains filed for bankruptcy between 1958 and 1969.[134] The modest chain was not immune to outside financial forces. Second, Taylor Son & Company leaned on May Company for its growth capital. It had no real access to larger pools of capital and was quite dependent on May to make the significant financial decisions. May had all the control over Taylor. Finally, the downtown areas in many cities were becoming less and less of a destination for shoppers given the proliferation of retail shops and malls in the suburbs. This was especially true in Cleveland. Located near East Ninth Street, Taylor's had steadily lost customers after interurban trains and transit traffic were rerouted from East Ninth to the Terminal Tower. Higbee's and May's were picking up that business.

On October 30, 1961, the May Company announced the closing of the Taylor Son & Company historic downtown store. The department store's Southgate branch was converted to a May Company store. The iconic Taylor Son & Company was no more, a victim to the changing demographics of the early 1960s. The closure of the store had a tremendous effect on downtown

Patrons shopping at Taylor Department Store (1961).

Cleveland. Many historians and economists privy to the wealth and the woes of Cleveland often note the closing of Taylor & Son's as the beginning of a long and desperate slide of downtown Cleveland's fortunes.

In 1964, Albert Levin, a Cleveland-based real estate developer, acquired the property from May Company and remodeled it into an office building named the 666 Euclid Building. The opening of the site as an office building did offer street-level retail, as a Gray Drugstore and a Lerner clothing shop were built out.

Levin sold the building in the early 1980s. The new owner updated the office complex and renamed the building the Atrium Office Plaza. It became increasingly difficult to lease office space in the building, and over the years, it turned into a blighted eyesore on Euclid Avenue. The building was sold in 1995 and again in 1998 with little progress being made in terms of tenants and profitability. By 2007, the once glamorous Taylor Building stood empty.

Today, the Taylor Son & Company department store building is experiencing a bit of a renaissance. The entire building has been redeveloped as apartments and some corporate offices. On June 3, 2008,

Southgate entrance to William Taylor Department Store (1958).

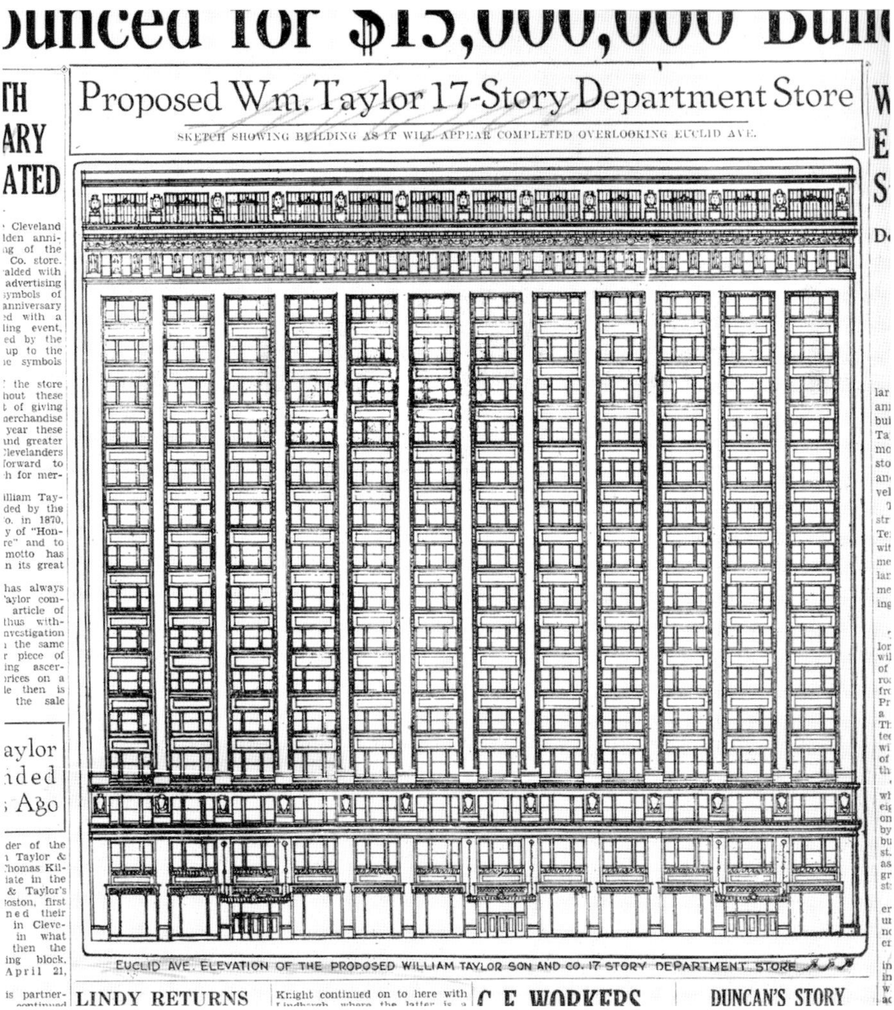

Above: A drawing of the proposed seventeen-story Taylor Department Store to be on Euclid Avenue (1928).

Opposite, top: The hustle and bustle of Cleveland in front of the Taylor Department Store on Euclid Avenue (1934).

Opposite, bottom: People eating at the Taylor Department Store restaurant (1961).

Taylor Department Store celebrates its twenty-sixth "birthday" at its Euclid Avenue location (1941).

it was announced that Willoughby, Ohio–based developer K&D Group had acquired the old Taylor Son & Company building, an attached garage and the Dollar Bank Building for $16.2 million. The Dollar Bank Building was torn down, and the Taylor Son & Company building was renovated as an apartment complex with 240 units and sixty-five thousand square feet of office space. A restaurant, Hodge's, was opened on the street level of the building. The restaurant was a partnership between Chef Chris Hodgson, who appeared on *The Great Food Truck Race* show on Food Network, and Scott Kuhn, owner of numerous restaurants in Cleveland, including Washington Place Bistro and 87 West Wine Bar. The total cost of the redevelopment for the former Taylor's department store building was nearly $70 million. The building's redevelopment has been a tremendous success and has been a key component to downtown Cleveland's revival.

The Characters

Sophia Strong Taylor

Taylor was one of America's top businesswomen at a time when there were so few active women in the retail sector. Sophia Strong Taylor was born on May 5, 1861, in Mexico, Missouri. Her family moved to Cleveland in 1870 searching for better fortunes. In 1890, Sophia married J. Livingston Taylor. Taylor was the scion of the William Taylor Son & Company. J. Livingston died two years after their marriage, and Sophia was given ownership of the company.

Her management style was guided by moral and religious principles. A dominant figure in the mercantile life of the city, she was also a leader in religious and philanthropic activities. Following her husband's death in 1892, she served as president of William Taylor Son & Company until 1935, when she became chairman of the board. She gave liberally to Presbyterian missions, the Community Fund and other philanthropies. A large part of her estate in Bratenahl, named Taylorhurst, was converted to homes for

A father and daughter having fun playing in the toy department at Taylor & Sons (1961).

Chef Ignatz Debelyak, chef at Taylor's Southgate, supervises the elaborate buffet served every Wednesday at Taylor's Southgate store (1959).

Taylor Kilpatrick & Company on South Ontario Street and Public Square (1879). *Courtesy of Weztler's Photography.*

The Walker & Weeks architectural design for a new Taylor Department Store on Euclid Avenue (1927). *Courtesy of Western Reserve Historical Society.*

crippled and needy children. She insisted on a strict Sabbath observance, and, traditionally, no Sunday advertising was used and curtains of show windows were drawn on the Sabbath until 1939.

She passed away on September 25, 1936. On the day of her funeral, William Taylor Son & Company was closed. She was beloved by her employers and respected by her retail competitors.

NOTES

Preface

1. James Wallers, *Cleveland's Golden Story* (Cleveland: William Taylor Son & Co., 1920). Published to commemorate the Golden Jubilee of the William Taylor Son & Co.
2. Mike Campbell, "Meaning, Origin and History of the Name Euclid," www.behindthename.com/name/euclid.
3. Herbert H. Harwood, *Invisible Giants: The Empires of Van Sweringen Brothers* (Bloomington: Indiana University Press, 2003).
4. Carol Poh Miller, "Historic and Architectural Resources of the Lower Prospect/Huron District of Cleveland, Ohio," National Register of Historic Places Continuation Sheet, September 9, 1992, E-5-h-13, Cleveland Landmarks Commission Submission.
5. James M. Wood, *Halle's: Memoirs of a Family Department Store* (n.p.: Geranium Press, 1987).
6. Laura DeMarco, "Cleveland Christmas Memories," Cleveland.com, November 30, 2017, www.cleveland.com.
7. Marci Rich, "Remembering the Silver Grille," Huffington Post, June 8, 2013, www.huffingtonpost.com.
8. Karin Connelly Rice, "Re-Emergence: Nostalgic Higbee's Space Is to Let," FreshWater, April 26 2017, www.freshwatercleveland.com.
9. "Sterling-Linder Company," Wikipedia, www.wikipedia.org.
10. Richard E. Karberg, et al., *A Higbee History: From Designer Labels to Casino Tables* (n.p.: Cleveland Landmarks Press, Inc., 2014).

The Bailey Company

11. William Ganson Rose, *Cleveland: The Making of a City*, 2nd ed. (Kent, OH: Kent State University Press, 1990). Previously published by the World Publishing Company in 1950.
12. Ibid.
13. Rachel Verba, "Bailey's Department Store," Cleveland Historical, May15, 2015, www.clevelandhistorical.org.
14. Rose, *Cleveland.*
15. John E. Bryan, "Youngstown Firm Buys Bailey Co," *Plain Dealer*, June 12, 1956.
16. Mark J. Price, "Westgate Shopping Center Welcomed 'Store of the Century' in July 1952," *Akron Beacon Journal*, July 10, 2017, www.ohio.com.
17. Richard Klein, "'Let's Go Shopping at the Square': Cleveland's Leading Downtown Department Stores: A Business Legacy," Cleveland Memory, 2014, engagedscholarship.csuohio.edu/clevmembks/25.
18. "May's Starts Razing Old Bailey Co. Store," *Cleveland Press*, April 18, 1963.
19. "Bailey's to Close Downtown Store, E. 101st Outlet," *Cleveland Press*, February 14, 1962.
20. Rose, *Cleveland.*
21. "Now We Start," *Lakewood Post*, April 10, 1930.
22. Dan Chalk, "Big Stores Once Thrived in City," Lakewood Historical Society, February 2, 2019, www.lakewoodhistory.org. Originally published in the *Lakewood Sun Post*, June 28, 1990.
23. Ibid.
24. "Bailey's Lakewood Remodeling Typical of Many Others," *Lakewood Post*, April 14, 1955.
25. "Expansion Project Transforms Bailey's Store in Lakewood," *Plain Dealer*, Bailey Company Special Section, November 29, 1964.
26. "Nevilles $200,000 Expansion Will Extend Store into New INA Building," *Lakewood Post*, February 3, 1966.
27. "Colonel Louis Black," Encyclopedia of Cleveland History, Case Western Reserve University, case.edu/ech.
28. Mark J. Price, "Westgate Shopping Center Welcomed 'Store of the Century' in July 1952," Ohio.com, July 10, 2017.

Halle Bros. Company

29. "Halle Brothers Co.," Encyclopedia of Cleveland History, Case Western Reserve University, case.edu/ech.
30. Wood, *Halle's.*
31. Rose, *Cleveland.*
32. Wood, *Halle's.*
33. Michael C. DeAloia, *Lost Grand Hotels of Cleveland* (Charleston, SC: The History Press, 2014).
34. Wood, *Halles.*
35. Ibid.
36. Jim Dubelko, "The John Hartness Complex," Cleveland Historical, www.clevelandhistorical.org.
37. Ibid.
38. Stan Bullard, "Euclid Avenue Eyesore Set for Renovation," *Crain's Cleveland Business*, October 2, 2018, www.crainscleveland.com.
39. Lorrie K. Owen, ed., *Dictionary of Ohio Historic Places*, vol. 1 (n.p.: Somerset Publishers, Inc., 1990).
40. "Halle Building," Wikipedia, www.wikipedia.org.
41. Wood, *Halle's.*
42. Ibid.
43. Tim Trepal and Kelsey Smith, "Penitentiary Glen: The Halle Farm," Cleveland Historical, May 31, 2012, www.clevelandhistorical.org.
44. Jim Dubelko, "The Salmon Halle Mansion," Cleveland Historical, May 31, 2012, clevelandhistorical.org/items/show/424.
45. Harwood, *Invisible Giants.*
46. "Interurban," Wikipedia, www.wikipedia.org.
47. Eric Johannesen, *A Cleveland Legacy: The Architecture of Walker & Weeks* (Kent, OH: Kent State University Press, 1999). In cooperation with the Western Reserve Historical Society.
48. Christopher Busta-Peck, "In Search of Mr. Jingeling. Part One," Cleveland Area History, December 11, 2009, www.clevelandareahistory.com.
49. Herb Strawbridge, *Remembering Higbee's* (n.p.: Western Reserve Historical Society, 2004). Published with the support of the John P. Murphy Foundation.
50. "Manuel Halle,"Encyclopedia of Cleveland History, Case Western Reserve University, www.case.edu/ech. Extracted from *The History of Halle Bros. Company* by Edwin W. Crooks Jr. (1959).

51. Ibid.
52. "Salmon Portland Halle," Encyclopedia of Cleveland History, Case Western Reserve University, case.edu/ech.
53. Wood, *Halle's*.
54. James M. Wood, *Out & About with Winsor French* (Kent, OH: Kent State University Press, 2011).
55. "Walter M. Halle; Headed Store Chain," *New York Times*, January 11, 1972.
56. "Kay Halle Personal Papers," JFK Library, Presidential Libraries, www.jfklibrary.org.
57. J.Y. Smith, "Kay Halle, Washington Grande Dame, Dies at 93," *Washington Post*, August 12, 1997, www.washingtonpost.com/archives.
58. Robert McG. Thomas, "Kay Halle an Intimate of Century's Giants," *New York Times*, August 24, 1997.
59. "Halle Brothers Co.," Wikipedia, www.wikipedia.org.

Higbee's

60. "Abram Garfield," Encyclopedia of Cleveland History, Case Western Reserve University, www.case.edu/ech.
61. "Abram Garfield," Wikipedia, www.wikipedia.org.
62. Richard E. Karberg, et al., *A Higbee History: From Designer Labels to Casino Tables* (n.p.: Cleveland Landmarks Press, Inc., 2014).
63. Michael C. DeAloia, *Lost Cleveland: Seven Wonders of the Sixth City* (Charleston, SC: The History Press, 2010).
64. Encyclopedia of Cleveland History, Case Western Reserve University, www.ech.cwru.edu.
65. Debbi Snook, "The Great Lakes Exposition. Boxing Cats, Aquadudes and a 90-Pound Sturgeon," *Plain Dealer Magazine*, June 2, 1991.
66. Strawbridge, *Remembering Higbee's*.
67. Ibid.
68. "Joseph Horne Company," Wikipedia, www.wikipedia.org.
69. Strawbridge, *Remembering Higbee's*.
70. Karberg, *Higbee History*.
71. Ibid.
72. Amanda Garrett, "Lovely Secrets of Terminal Tower," Plain Dealer News Archive, August 27, 2011, www.cleveland.com.
73. Strawbridge, *Remembering Higbee's*.

74. "John P. Murphy," Encyclopedia of Cleveland History, Case Western Reserve University, case.edu/ech.
75. "About John & Gladys Murphy," John P. Murphy Foundation, Murphy Kulas, www.murphykulas.org.
76. George E. Condon, *Cleveland: The Best Kept Secret* (New York: Doubleday & Company, 1967).
77. D.D. Van Tassel and J.J. Grabowski, *The Dictionary of Cleveland Biography* (Bloomington: Indiana University Press, 1996).
78. Harwood, *Invisible Giants.*
79. Ibid.
80. Van Tassel and Grabowski, *Dictionary of Cleveland Biography.*
81. Condon, *Cleveland: The Best Kept Secret.*
82. Eric Johannesen, *Cleveland Architecture: 1876–1976* (Cleveland, OH: Western Reserve Historical Society, 1979).
83. Ibid.
84. Teresa Garcia, "Iconic Skyscraper to Bring New Housing to Downtown Cleveland," *Journal of Tax Credits* 9, no. 9 (September 2018): 1–6, www.novoco.com.
85. "Terminal Tower," Wikipedia, www.wikipedia.org.
86. Rose, *Cleveland.*
87. Harwood, *Invisible Giants.*
88. Ibid.
89. Ibid.
90. Condon, *Cleveland: The Best Kept Secret.*
91. Harwood, *Invisible Giants.*

May Company

92. Gillian Wolf, "The May Department Stores Company," Encyclopedia.com, 2006. Updated by Laura E. Whiteley.
93. Klein, "'Let's Go Shopping at the Square.'
94. Owen, *Dictionary of Ohio Historic Places.*
95. "May Company," Cleveland Historical, July 1, 2011, clevelandhistorical.org/items/show/241.
96. "An Indoor Playground in the Downtown May Company Store," Cleveland.com, Advance Ohio, October 12, 2011, www.cleveland.com.
97. Arlene Fine, "Recalling the May Days of Cleveland Past," *Cleveland Jewish News*, September 22, 2006, www.clevelandjewishnews.com/archives.

98. Klein, "'Let's Go Shopping at the Square.'"
99. Wolf, "May Department Stores Company."
100. Klein, "'Let's Go Shopping at the Square.'"
101. Rose, *Cleveland*.
102. Ibid.
103. Klein, "'Let's Go Shopping at the Square.'"
104. "May Company Ohio," Wikipedia, www.wikipedia.org.
105. Klein, "'Let's Go Shopping at the Square.'"
106. "May Company Ohio," Wikipedia.
107. "Kaufmann's—A Division of the May Department Stores Company," Encyclopedia of Cleveland History, Case Western Reserve University, case.edu/ech.
108. Klein, "'Let's Go Shopping at the Square.'"
109. "The May Department Stores Company," Wikipedia, www.wikipedia.org.
110. John Kosich, "Once the Third Largest Store in US, Historic May Co. Building on Public Square No Longer Ignored," News 5 Cleveland, May 24, 2018, www.news5cleveland.com.
111. "Restoring the May Company Building's White Terra Cotta Façade," *Boston Valley Terra Cotta*, January 3, 2019, bostonvalley.com.
112. Van Tassel and Grabowski, *Dictionary of Cleveland Biography*.
113. Rose, *Cleveland*.

Sterling Linder Davis Department Store

114. "Sterling-Linder Company," Encyclopedia of Cleveland History, Case Western Reserve University, case.edu/ech.
115. Van Tassel and Grabowski, *Dictionary of Cleveland Biography*.
116. Walter B. Henderson and Holly R. Witchey, "The Ark," Encyclopedia of Cleveland History, Case Western Reserve University, www.case.edu/ech.
117. "J. Milton Dyer," Wikipedia, www.wikipedia.org.
118. Samuel Peter Orth, *A History of Cleveland, Ohio* (n.p.: S.J. Clarke Publishing Co., 1910).
119. Rose, *Cleveland*.
120. "Lydia May Ames," Encyclopedia of Cleveland History, Case Western Reserve University, case.edu/ech.
121. Rose, *Cleveland*.

122. "Linda McCartney," Wikipedia, www.wikipedia.org.
123. Owen, *Dictionary of Ohio Historic Places*.
124. Klein, "'Let's Go Shopping at the Square.'"
125. Ibid.
126. Stan Bullard, "Distressed Downtown Cleveland Office Building Gets New Owner," *Crain's Cleveland Business*, February 22, 2016, www.crainscleveland.com.
127. "H. Black & Company Building," Wikipedia, www.wikipedia.org.
128. "Morris Alfred Black," Encyclopedia of Cleveland History, Case Western Reserve University, www.case.edu/ech.

William Taylor Son & Company

129. Van Tassel and Grabowski, *Dictionary of Cleveland Biography*.
130. Rose, *Cleveland*.
131. Johannesen, *Cleveland Legacy*.
132. Klein, "'Let's Go Shopping at the Square.'"
133. Ibid.
134. Ibid.

ABOUT THE AUTHOR

Although not a native Clevelander, Michael is known for his deep love and knowledge of the "Sixth City." The best things in his life, both personally and professionally, have happened while living in Cleveland. He is currently the chief executive officer of the Evergreen Podcasts, a media company that produces podcasts and other on-demand broadcast programming.

Michael is perhaps best known for his term at the City of Cleveland as the senior executive for technology development, or "Tech Czar," where he was responsible for the economic development of the technology industries in the city. During his tenure as the "Tech Czar," Michael was able to recruit thirty-seven tech companies into the city of Cleveland, which brought or created many much-needed jobs to the city and revenue to other city businesses. It was during this time that he became intimately knowledgeable on a large number of downtown Cleveland buildings, including the various retail palaces detailed in this book.

He is the former tech columnist for the *Plain Dealer* and past co-host of *Cleveland Confidential Radio*. Michael was also the regional vice president for the Cleveland operations of Expedient, a Pittsburgh, Pennsylvania–based data center business. Michael was also the co-founder and chief financial officer of BlueBridge Networks, a Cleveland-based provider of data center services. Michael also co-founded EmergingChefs.com, a Cleveland-based culinary event and content company.

Michael also worked for LNE Group; FIT Technologies; Saltz, Shamis & Goldfarb; Ernst & Young; and National City Venture Capital. Currently, Michael is an investor and board member at Metisentry, an Akron-based software development company, and Junto, a Cleveland-based mobile application developer.

He has appeared on the Fox News channel's *John Stoessel Show*. He has been featured in two documentary films, the Drew Carey–produced Reason Foundation documentary titled *Reason Saves Cleveland* (2012) and the Socent Studios film *Rust Belt Renaissance* (2018).

Michael earned his MBA from Case Western Reserve University and his bachelor's degree from Xavier University. He is the author of *Lost Cleveland*, a short history of some of the leading architectural wonders of Cleveland, which was published by The History Press in late 2010, and *Lost Grand Hotels of Cleveland*, which was published by The History Press in 2014. He currently lives in Lakewood, Ohio, with his wife, Nora, and their young daughter, Ileana.